# PRESSING INTO POWERFUL

# PRAYER

## PRAYERS FOR
## SUPERNATURAL BREAKTHROUGHS

# THERESA CRICHLOW

THE EARNEST (HEARTFELT, CONTINUED) PRAYER OF A RIGHTEOUS MAN
MAKES TREMENDOUS POWER AVAILABLE [DYNAMIC IN ITS WORKING]

JAMES 5:16

©2020, **Pressing into Powerful Prayer**
Theresa Crichlow

New York, NY
Direct: 1-862-231-5103
Website: https://theresacrichlow.com
Email: theresaministries@gmail.com

Published by
Anointed Fire House
www.anointedfirehouse.com

ISBN: 978-1-7354654-4-9

# FOREWORD

*2 Chronicles 7:14*
*If my people, which are called by my name, shall humble themselves, and pray, and seek my face, and turn from their wicked ways; then will I hear from Heaven, and will forgive their sin, and will heal their land.*

The Word of God encourages us to call upon His name, humble ourselves and pray. Yet, there are so many people who struggle with praying. The least attended service in the local church is normally prayer, and most believers are never taught how to approach the throne of God.

While prayer, in its simplest form, is having intimate conversations with Father God, there are yet many complexities in prayer. In Luke 11:1, Christ's disciples asked Him to teach them to pray. At that time, He gave them the model prayer as a pattern to shape their communion with Father God. What I find interesting is that when they approached Him, they made reference to the point John had also taught his followers to pray. This pattern of prayer should have continued in the modern church as well.

Too often, the concept of prayer is only to take our desires to God so He can make us happy by answering us immediately with a yes. We forget or just don't know that we are to enter into a relationship with God, and therefore, our time spent with Him should be a two-way conversation. Not only that, but it is more important to hear from Him than to tell Him what we need. Isaiah 65:24 teaches us that before we ask, He will answer us. In other words, He already knows your needs. Yes, He does still want us to bring our cares to Him, but we must also be mindful of what He desires to release into the Earth realm as well.

Prayer strategies are found in God's Word. The exceptionality of this book is that Prophetess Theresa Crichlow has given the reader foundational truths found in the Word of God to build upon as they learn how to pray. Intercession is not just her calling; it is woven in the very fiber of her being. She has given herself to the Lord in a way that many aren't willing to do. What God has revealed to her, she is willing to share with others.

This book is a must have in every intercessor's library. As you embark upon the journey of prayer found on these pages, I encourage you to have a pen and paper handy as God will speak to you through these teachings. I rejoice in knowing that you are about to encounter God in a whole new way. Enjoy your intimate time with your Creator!!

**Elder Coylette James**
Coylette James Ministries
www.coylettejames.org

# DECISION PAGE

Before you proceed to pray these Anointed Prayers, may I invite you to accept Jesus Christ as Lord and Savior over your life if you are not saved?

The Bible says, "That if thou shalt confess with thy mouth the Lord Jesus and shalt believe in thy heart that God hath raised Him from the dead, thou shalt be saved. For with the heart man believeth unto righteousness; and with the mouth confession is made unto salvation" (Romans 10:9-10).

## PRAY THIS PRAYER WITH ME TODAY

Father God, I thank You for sending Your Son Jesus to die for my sins. I believe that Jesus died for me and rose again from the dead for my justification. I confess to You that I am a sinner and I cannot save myself. I ask that You forgive me of my sins and wash me with the blood of Jesus. I accept You as my Lord and personal Savior. Jesus, come into my heart and make me a new creature, according to Your Word. Write my name in the Lamb's Book of Life. I thank You, Jesus, for saving and accepting me into Your eternal Kingdom. I will live for You and I will walk in Your peace and joy from this day forward, in Jesus' name. Amen. May God richly bless you in your new-found life in Him.

I would like to read this message with your undivided attention. However, before you go on, I would like you to pray these prayer points with all the breath that you can muster. By the time you would have finished reading this message, a divine exchange will have taken place in your life. The change that you will experience will make even your enemies wonder. This means that the powers that have been sitting on your breakthroughs, whether they are physical, emotional, financial, relational, professional, or in every realm will all of a sudden somersault.

Also, after reading this message, there will be an overturning and overtaking. When the crisis starts, the purpose will be to bring you favor. Also, long-term problems shall be disgraced.

I want you to pull down the clouds of your breakthroughs by saying, "O Heavens, release my breakthroughs, in the Name of Jesus. Psalm 124:7 says, 'Our soul is escaped as a bird out of the snare of the fowlers: the snare is broken, and we are escaped.'"

The first thing I would like you to know is the fact that God is not a failure, therefore, His children should not be a failure in any way. God did not design anyone to come into this world and fail. Any failure we find in our lives is not the fault of God.

## MANIFESTED FAVOR

The Lord is my Shepherd, I will not lack because the Father of Glory has chosen me to be blessed with all spiritual blessings, and has seated me in Heavenly places. My Lord and my King, search me through and remove those things that offend You and cause me to stumble, as I repent for all of the sins, transgressions, and iniquities in my life and my family line.

As a new creation in Christ Jesus and Your offspring of grace, I ask for Your manifested favor to surround me all the days of my life, according to Your will. Correct the mistakes, errors, and decisions that have interrupted Your favor from being expressed and multiplied in my projects, finances, health and relationships. Allow me to be a witness and testimony of Your life-giving power and supernatural favor. Let me serve as a sign and wonder to express Your love, along with expanding and advancing Your Kingdom in the Earth. You instructed us to ask, seek, and know You. Let it be done unto me as a covenant servant for Your glory, in Jesus' name. Amen.

# TABLE OF CONTENTS

# INTRODUCTION

Prayer is one of the greatest assets of the redeemed. It is our communication link with God, our Heavenly Father. Unfortunately, however, many are either not taking advantage of this privilege or they approach it wrongly. No wonder you hear some people say, "I have exhausted prayer, yet there is no breakthrough." James 4:2-3 tells us the reason for their failure: "You lust and have not: you kill, and desire to have, and cannot obtain: you fight and war, yet you have not, because you ask not. You ask and do not receive because you ask amiss." Until you know the meaning of prayer and how to pray correctly, you will never be free from the pressures of life.

This powerful prayer book was birthed out of my own personal prayer vigil in pursuit of the manifest presence of God, and to go deeper in revelation, worship, and my love for Him. It includes prayers that have transformed many lives, and these prayers will transform your life too. This book also includes prayers that will bring God's will to Earth as it is in Heaven. And because these prayers are to be prayed regularly, you will become skilled in the Word of righteousness (Hebrews 5:13) and will begin speaking as the oracles of God (1 Peter 4:11).

Prayer is not just communication. It is having the correct approach to communicating with God, because it takes praying aright to be heard. The Kingdom of God is a Kingdom of principles. Everything is expected to be done according to the guidelines of the Word; otherwise, it will yield no profit. This is why Jesus laid down the right principles for effectual and winning prayers in Mathew 6. "After this manner therefore pray ye: Our Father which art in Heaven, Hallowed be thy name. Thy Kingdom come. Thy will be done in Earth, as it is in Heaven. Give us this day our daily bread. And forgive us our debtors. And lead us not into temptation, but deliver us from evil: For thine is the Kingdom, and the power, and the glory, forever. Amen" (Mathew 6:9-13).

This is the prototype for effectual prayer; it is a failure-proof prayer guide. When you get it right, the guess-work stops and you are assured of answers, even before you are through praying. There are certain things in life that you will never enjoy, except through the proper use of communication with Heaven. Jesus said:

> "For every one that asked received; and he that seeks finds; and to him that knocked it shall be opened" (Mathew 7:8).

Certain doors in life will never open to you until you properly engage your communication link with God. There are many things that are rightfully yours in God's covenant, but you may never enjoy them until you ask, seek and knock correctly.

When I gave my heart to Jesus many years ago, I was told three things I must do in order to grow in the grace and power of God. The first was continuous prayer, the second was praise and worship, and the third was reading and meditating on the Word of God. I took it literally. I would pray in my home, in the supermarket, on the job, and everywhere I went (besides church). I would "try" to sing (*smiles*) and worship, and I would read and meditate on the Word of God. Lastly, I would memorize scriptures. So I became a lover of the Word of God. I would write them on postcards and tape them throughout my house.

Prayer requires no other treatment in Heaven than answers. God has no record book for prayers, neither does He have a storeroom for them. They are either answered or returned to the sender. That is the reason many have never received answers to their prayers. But from now on, be sure to use this powerful prayer book so that every time you stand before God in prayer, you will always receive answers.

I still remember, as if it were yesterday, my first encounter with the manifested presence of God. It was several weeks after I got saved. I was very desperate to know God. One evening, I was praying in my living room when all of a sudden, an overshadowing presence invaded the room and enveloped me. I had a visitation and I was elated. It seemed as if I was standing in Heavenly dew. The presence was so heavy that all I could do was weep. While I was basking in this glory, the scripture came to mind that says "God is a rewarder of them that diligently seek Him." This paired with the scripture where God says, "If you will seek me with all your heart, with all your strength, with all your soul, you will find me." All I did was just seek Him, praise Him, worship Him, and love Him. I gave God my all to the best of my ability. God is true to His Word; He showed up.

Prayer is the breath of the regenerated Spirit. Just like every strong relationship thrives on the maintenance of a very good communication link between the parties involved, prayer not only serves as a means of getting God to intervene in our affairs, it enhances the strength of our relationship with Him, since it is one of the ways we fellowship with Him.

Prayer is not optional for the believer because it is one of our vital covenant responsibilities. This is why the Word of God admonishes us to pray always. "And he speaks a parable to them to this end, that men ought to pray always, and not to faint" (Luke 18:1). "Pray without ceasing" (1 Thessalonians 5:17).

There is power in prayer. Prayer is the key that opens the door to the storehouses of God's grace, power, blessing, and more glory. *Hallelujah!* Through the power of prayer and faith, men of old subdued Kingdoms, obtained promises, stopped the mouth of lions, quenched the violence of fire, escaped the edge of the sword, put death on hold, cured diseases, rescued cities from destruction, stopped plagues, stopped the sun in its course, strengthened weak men, made some invincible in battle, brought down fire from Heaven, unlocked the cabinet of the womb, brought the dead back to life, shut and unlocked the floodgates of rain, and forced open the prison's doors as well as the iron gates.

When your soul is genuinely revived, prayer becomes a God-given privilege that you cannot afford to abuse; instead, you'll make the utmost use of it. It naturally becomes a part of your life, because your spirit has been attuned to crave communication with God, as a newborn babe craves for milk.

When the first Church was born, the apostles said: "But we will give ourselves continually to prayer, and to the ministry of the word" (Act 6:4).
That was how they were able to sustain the fire in their days. Whenever they prayed, there were undeniable proofs that they'd touched Heaven (Acts 4:23-31, 16:25-26). When your prayer life begins to drag, it means that your spirit-man is already drooping. This means you are getting further and further away from God. Consistent, effectual prayer is the way to maintain a high-flying Christian life.

Anyone can pray, but few pray with power! What is it that changes standard prayers into powerful prayers? The answer is fasting. Fasting enhances our prayer life and gives us an immediate victory over the devil. For example, there's the account of the disciples trying to cast a devil out of a demon-possessed boy. "Afterward, the disciples came to Jesus and asked Him privately, 'Why could not we cast him out?'" Jesus told them the secret to spiritual power. He said, "This kind can only come out by prayer and fasting." When facing difficult situations, circumstances, strongholds, generational curses, perpetual lack, chronic pain, terminal diseases, and ungodly occurrences, you need to add some fasting to your prayer regime. This will allow you to see longstanding strongholds crumble before your eyes, if it be His will. John Wesley believed so much in fasting that he refused to ordain young men into the ministry who would not fast two days out of a week.

Prayer flies on two wings, and that's praise and worship. The Psalmist David said, "Enter into His gates with thanksgiving and into His courts with praise. Be thankful to Him, and bless His name" (Psalm 100-4). Prayer is our lifeline, prayer is our lifeblood, and praise is as essential to a powerful prayer life as air is to breathing. When we are in His presence, the next thing to do is to worship Him. Hallelujah! Worship brings forth God's glory. The glory of God will descend like dew, like the rain shower, like a gray or yellow smoke, and like fire in your prayer closet. It will descend in your home, while you're streaming live, and in the church (when He is truly worshiped). That glory of God will transform you from glory to glory. It transformed Moses so much that his face shown like the brightness of the sun, until the people could not behold his face. On the mount of transfiguration, the disciples saw a strange glow on Jesus' face as He continued in prayer. That strange glow was nothing else but the Glory of God. *Hallelujah*! That glory will overshadow you, envelope you, permeate you, and saturate you until you are highly charged and fully clothed with the power of God. When you walk into a room, demons will start to flee through the windows, and when you walk into a place full of demoniacs, witches and wizards, they will start to act funny. This will happen if you will give yourself to prayer.

There is more to prayer than just praying. In my early Christian days, we all prayed because we saw others praying. No one was mindful of results, so we continued to tarry until many got tired and some eventually retired. It is therefore very important that we know what benefits prayer holds for us as believers, and how to use them to our advantages so we can enjoy a victorious Christian life.

What is the use of calling a number on the phone, not getting through and then, giving your message to the blank phone waves? It's nothing but wasted efforts. A very religious man, rather than drop the handset when he can't get through, will still go on to say, "Though I know you are not picking up the phone, I am going to say everything I have to say anyway, because I know you will hear me someday." That is exactly what we do when we don't apply the correct prayer principles.

Persistence and perseverance are very impactful in prayer. You must have heated prayer. Half-hearted prayers have no place at the throne of God. For example, Elijah's persistent prayers for rain caused the rain clouds to appear above the horizon. Daniel pressed his case to the courts of fairness for three weeks before the answer, the breakthrough, and the blessing finally came. Jesus spent many nights in prayer in Gethsemane. He presented the same petition three times with urgent and obedient persistence. The widow's persistence granted her the justice she desired. Blind Bartimaeus' persistence helped him to win, even in the face of opposition when he was being rebuked from the surrounding crowd. His mat was not his mate. His persistence won where half-hearted indifference would surely have failed.

The very essence of passionately praying is a burdened heart or a soul crying and travailing before God. Prayers that come from a broken heart are the most powerful forms of prayer ever known. Prayers that do not move you will not move God. 2 Kings 22:19 reads, "'Because your heart was tender and you humbled yourself before the Lord when you heard what I spoke against this place and against its inhabitants, that they would become desolation and a curse, and you tore your clothes and wept in my presence, I also have heard you,' says the Lord."

Redemption gives us all equal access to God's hotline, but many are missing out on it because of their lack of understanding. They don't know how to approach it. God said, "My people are destroyed for lack of knowledge," not for lack of prayers.

Prayer is also a weapon with which we do battle and contend with our opposition; this is so that we can possess our inheritance in Christ. But it is not just enough to have a weapon in your hand, you must have a sound understanding of how it operates. That way, you won't become a victim, but a victor in battle.

It is my prayer that this powerful prayer book will achieve that purpose in your life and deliver to you the secrets for a winning prayer life. From henceforth, you will emerge a winner each time you engage the force of prayer, in Jesus' name.
Amen.

# WORSHIP GOD THE FATHER

### *Psalm 34:3*
### *O magnify the Lord with me, and let us exalt His name together.*

1. Great and mighty God, I come to magnify and exalt Your holy name. I come to bow before Your Majesty. My Father, who art in Heaven, hallowed be Your name.
2. It's only because of Your extravagant love and amazing grace that I can even consider coming into Your presence.
3. God, I give thanks to You, Almighty King, in the Great Congregation. I give You a worthy praise. I will exalt Thee among the people because of Your goodness to me in the land of the living. You have delivered my soul from death and my feet from falling, therefore, I bless You.
4. Bless the Lord, O my soul, and all that is within me; bless His holy name and forget not His benefits. You are the Father of lights and the Giver of only good and perfect gifts.
5. For You alone are God; besides You, there is no other. You are the Creator of all things. You are the God of Abraham, God of Isaac and God of Jacob. Holy and Awesome, You are God!

6. You are the God who sits on the throne of the universe. You dwell between the cherubim and seraphim. You clothe Yourself with light like with a garment. You inhabit eternity.

7. Your name is Jehovah-Yahweh, Jehovah-Nissi. Jehovah-Stidkenu. You are Jehovah-Shallom, Jehovah-Adonai, and Jehovah-Rohi.

8. You are the God of our victory, Jehovah Nissi, my great banner, and I call You faithful during what seems so inexplicable.

9. Great mercies! Everlasting kindness! Covenant of peace! Precious promises to the believers from no one less than the Almighty God!

10. You are the one who pledges by no other name than "I Am."

11. You are not in our yesterday; Your name is not "I was." You are not in our worries about tomorrow; Your name is not "I will be."

12. You are our ever-present God, "I Am That I Am."

13. There is no way You are going to let our last chapter be less than our first chapter; the glory of the latter house shall be greater than the glory of the former house.

14. There are benefits in giving You glory. You make Yourself evident to all who commit to worship You. You become real and You become present to everyone who seeks You.

15. God, You have made me to sit in Heavenly places, far above all principalities and powers. As I align my

position with Yours, greater will be my ability to overcome.

16. You are the Great and Terrible God.

17. You are the Custodian of Life, breath and soul.

18. You pardon those You preserve as Your remnants.

19. Lord of Victory, the God of breakthrough, and the Warrior God. You are the God of the Breakthrough. You are the God of the Breaker. You are the One who breaks through for Your people. The Breaker goes ahead of the rest and hits the opposition first. You are a mighty yoke breaker!

20. The immortal and invisible God. You are Jehovah-Shammah, Jehovah-El-Shaddai, and Jehovah-Elyon.

21. The omnipresent, omnipotent and omniscient God. You are Jehovah-Rapha, Jehovah-Jireh, and Jihovah-Ropheka.

22. You are the Alpha and Omega, the God who has no beginning nor end. Jehovah-Elohim. Jehovah-Sabaoth. The I AM that I AM.

23. You are the God who preserves Your covenant and mercy with them who love You and keep Your Word.

24. You are the most merciful, loving, kind, generous and compassionate God.

25. When I think of all the works Your hands have made, my soul cries, "How great Thou art, most excellent God!"

26. When I think of the sky, the firmament, You spread it forth like a curtain and hang it on no pillar. When I

think of the Earth, You spread it forth like a mat on the deep waters.

27. When I think of the sun that gives light to the children of men during the day, and the beautiful serene moon that gives light at night, I cannot help but wonder aloud, "O Lord, my God, how beautiful are the works of Your hands!"

28. When I think of the beautiful stars that dot the Heavens like diamonds, my soul rejoices and says "Who is like unto our God, the great God of wonders?"

29. When I think of the birds of the air, they have no farm nor barn, but You feed them everyday. Not even the little sparrow falls to the ground without You knowing about it.

30. When I think about the different species of fish in the seas, with their varying traits, instincts, shapes and forms, I say in my heart, "God, how marvelous is Your creation!"

31. When I think of the animals, both domestic and wild, including the elephant, the zebra in all its beauty, the leopard, the camels, the monkeys, the giraffes, and the numerous mammals, I say, "God, how excellent You are!"

32. When I think of the Atlantic, the Pacific and the Indian oceans, and when I think of Mount Everest, the trees, and the beautiful flowers of the field, I say, "Who is like unto Thee, O God?!"

33. Above all wonders, when I think of how a baby grows in the womb of its mother, with its hands, eyes, feet, mouth, nose and ears, I say, "What an awesome God we serve!"

34. You are the Father in whom is all things. Let everything that has breath praise the Lord. Let the domestic and wild animals, the fish in the seas, the birds of the air, the trees, the mountains, the twenty-four elders and the holy angels join me now in praising the name of our God and our Maker. He is Lord of all. He is a Wonder. I say to everything that has breath, magnify the Lord with me; let us praise His name together.

35. To the only true and wise God be glory, honor, power, dominion, authority and all majesty forever and ever.

# Adoration to God the Father

In Christianity, God is known as God, the Father; God, our Father and God, the Father of Jesus. It is through these truths of relationship with our Creator that God is seen as the Father of all creatures and to all believers by grace.

Scripture says that the ways of God are "perfect" (Psalm 18:30), that He is "a faithful God who does nothing wrong" and that He is "righteous and just" (Deuteronomy 32: 4). This makes Him the perfect Father that You never had.

Maybe, you had a parent who was unapproachable, unloving, and who didn't have your best in mind. God, like the Heavenly Father He is, wants more than anything to make up for what you never had.

1. Merciful Father, we bless You. Thank You for being the King of glory. Thank You for being our Father, Redeemer, Shepherd and King. Thank You for reconciling us with Your Son, our Savior: Jesus Christ. We thank You for Your Holy Spirit who is the promised Intercessor and who enables us to be effective witnesses of His Kingdom here on Earth. Thank You for loving us and taking care of us.
2. Lord, let all that we are praise You. We will congratulate You as long as we live. We will sing Your

praises until the last breath. Our hope is in You, Lord, our God. You created the sky and the Earth, the sea and everything in them. You keep every promise forever. We are in awe of how amazing You are!

3. Beautiful Father, today we honor and exalt You. You are our God, and we represent our devotion and worship to You. You are the Alpha and the Omega, the Beginning and the End. You existed before time, and You created all that exists. Sir, You were just holding the ocean in Your hand. You have measured the sky with Your fingers and You know how much the Earth weighs! You are really amazing!

4. Great and mighty God, I come to glorify and exalt Your holy name. I come to worship in front of Your Majesty. My Father, who art in Heaven, Your name is hallowed.

5. God, I thank You, Almighty King, for the great fellowship. I thank You with dignity among the people for Your kindness to me in the land of the living. You delivered my soul from death and my feet from falling; therefore, I bless You.

6. Father, all the nations of the world are just a drop to You. It's just dust on the scales. You gather all the Earth as if it were a grain of sand!

7. Heavenly Father, You are seated on the circle of the Earth; the people below You are like grasshoppers. Spread the sky like curtains and make it Your tent. When we look at the sky, we know that You have created all the stars that we see. You take them out

like an army, one after the other, and You call them by name. Due to Your great and incomparable strength, nothing is missing. Lord, You are the Eternal God, the Creator of all the Earth. You never get weak or tired. No one can measure the depth of their understanding. You are good to everyone and You protect Your creation.

8. Mighty King, You are our Banner and our Shield, our Strength and our Protection. Lord Jesus, You are our Savior and our Redeemer, and through You, we are justified. Holy Spirit, You are our Advocate, our Helper, and the Source of our power. We honor You and love You, Triune God.

9. Almighty God, You reign! Lord, Your actions are great and wonderful! Your ways are kind and true, King of the people. Who will not fear and glorify Your name? You alone are holy! All the nations will come and worship before You, because righteous deeds have been revealed to You. In the name of Jesus. Amen.

10. Almighty Father, how wonderful You are! The mountain ranges reflect Your heights and the gentle valleys reflect Your grace. Almighty and Holy One, how creative You are! Every tree and every flower is full of wonder and generosity; every life resonates with subtleties and wonders. I will look to You, my magnificent, majestic and astonishing God.

11. I adore You, Father and Creator, hidden in the Blessed Sacrament. I adore You for all the works of Your hands, which reveal all wisdom, goodness and mercy,

Lord. You have spread so much beauty on Earth, and You have told me about Your beauty. Even though these beautiful things are only a small reflection of You, their beauty is incomprehensible because You are incomprehensible. And although You have hidden Your beauty, my eyes, illuminated by faith, reach out to You. My soul recognizes its Creator, it's Supreme God, and my heart is completely immersed in the prayer of worship of You.

12. My Father and Creator, Your kindness encourages me to speak to You. Your grace removes the abyss that separates You, the Creator from the creature. To speak to You, Lord, is the pleasure of my heart. In You, I find all that my heart can desire. Here, Your light illuminates my mind, allowing You to know Yourself more and more deeply. The currents of Your grace run through my heart. It is here that my soul draws eternal life.

13. Oh, my Father and my God, You alone give of Yourself and unite closely with Your wretched creature. O Father, may it be my greatest pleasure to see You love and proclaim Your praise and glory, especially the honor of Your grace.

# DAVID'S WORSHIP TO THE LORD

*1 Chronicles 29:10 -13*
*Therefore David blessed the Lord before all the assembly;*
*and David said: "Blessed are You, Lord God of Israel, our*
*Father, forever and ever.*

Yours, O Lord, is the greatness, the power and the glory, the victory and the majesty; for all that is in Heaven and in Earth is Yours. Yours is the Kingdom, O Lord, and You are exalted as head over all.
Both riches and honor come from You, and You reign over all. In Your hand is power and might; In Your hand is the power to make great and to give strength to all. Now therefore, our God, we thank You and praise Your glorious name.

## Daniel's Worship to God

*Daniel 2:20 -23*
*Daniel answered and said: "Blessed be the name of God*
*forever and ever, For wisdom and might are His.*

And He changes the times and the seasons; He removes kings and raises up kings; He gives wisdom to the wise and knowledge to those who have understanding.

He reveals deep and secret things; He knows what is in the darkness, and light dwells with Him.

I thank You and praise You, O God of my fathers. You have given me wisdom and might, and have now made known to me what we asked of You, for You have made known to us the king's demand."

| The Names of God | | |
|---|---|---|
| Psalm 110:1 | Jehovah-Yahweh | God of the universe |
| Genesis 17:1 | Jehovah-El Shadai | I Am Almighty God |
| Genesis 15:2,8 | Jehovah-Adonai | Sovereign Lord |
| Zechariah 14:5 | Jehovah-Elohay | The Lord My God |
| Exodus 20:2 | Jehovah-Eloheka | The Lord Your God |
| Genesis 2:4-25 | Jehovah-Elohim | Eternal Creator |
| Psalm 7:17 | Jehovah-Elyon | The Most High God |
| Psalm 95:6 | Jehovah-Hosenu | The Lord Our Maker |
| Genesis 22:8-14 | Jehovah-Jireh | The Great Provider |
| Leviticus 20:8 | Jehovah-Mekaddishkem | The Lord Our Sanctifier |
| Exodus 17:15 | Jehovah-Nissi | The Lord My Banner |

| Psalm 23:1 | Jehovah-Rohi | The Lord My Shepherd |
|---|---|---|
| Exodus 15:26 | Jehovah-Ropheka | The Lord My Healer |
| 1 Samuel 1:3 | Jehovah-Sabaothh | The Lord of Host |
| Judges 6:24 | Jehovah-Shalom | The Lord Our Peace |
| Ezekiel 48:35 | Jehovah-Shammah | The Lord is There |
| Jeremiah 23:6 | Jehovah-Tsidkenu | The Lord Our Righteousness |

# WORSHIP GOD THE SON

## Psalm 103:1
### Psalm of David. Bless the Lord, O my soul; and all that is within me, bless His holy name!

1. Lord Jesus, I come before You just to worship, adore and exalt Your wonderful name, the name that is above all names.

2. You are the King of kings and the Lord of lords, the Lion of the tribe of Judah, the Bright Morning Star, the Lily of the Valley, the Rose of Sharon, the Balm in Gilead, the Prince of Peace, Wonderful, Counselor and Son of the Most High God.

3. You are the Ancient of Days, the Rock of Ages, Alpha and Omega, the Beginning and End of all things, the Guardian and the Bishop of my soul, the Fairer than ten thousand.

4. You are the Miracle Worker, the great Physician and the Mighty Healer from Galilee, the Victor, the Conqueror, the Overcomer of all evil – Jesus, You are the same yesterday, today and forever.

5. You are the Way, the Truth and the Life. The Bread of Life, my Great Provider, Faithful and True Witness, the Captain and Commander-in-Chief of the armies of Heaven.

6. You are the Opener of hearts, the one who raises the

dead, the God of all hope. You are the one who delivered us from so great a death, who does deliver and will yet deliver. You are the one who calls, and the one who recompenses tribulation to all those who trouble us.

7. You are the Owner of the Kingdom, the one who spares life, pardons iniquity, passes by the transgression of Your remnant, and a Stronghold in the day of trouble.

8. You are a Friend who sticks closer than a brother, the Author and Finisher of my faith, my Redeemer, my Savior, my Deliverer, my Strong Tower, my Hiding Place – Jesus, the lover of my soul.

9. You are Emmanuel, God with us, Good Teacher, my Shepherd, Messiah, the Resurrection and the Life, the Author of Eternal salvation, the Ransom, Lamb without blemish, the Lamb of God, and the Holy One of Israel. You are Holy and unchanging. You are the Savior of the world.

10. You are the Great Shepherd of Israel, the Light of the world, the Maker of all things, the First Born among many brethren.

11. You are the one who comes with the Holy Spirit and Fire, Sanctifier, and the [soon] coming King.

12. To You alone belong all the glory, honor, power, authority, dominion, majesty and all excellencies forever and ever. Amen.

# ADORATION GOD THE SON

From eternity past, Jesus has always existed as God, the Son. Through Him all things were made.

### John 1:1-3
### *In the beginning was the Word, and the Word was with God, and the Word was God.*

He was with God in the beginning. Through Him, all things were made; without Him, nothing was made that has been made.

He has always existed in perfect relationship with God, the Father and God, the Holy Spirit. His role as God, the Son is not just a title that He's adopted during the course of His Earthly ministry, but a key aspect of His identity—an identity that always was and always will be.

1. Oh Christ, let me celebrate Your goodness and grace until the last moment of my life, with every drop of my blood and every beat of my heart. May I become Your hymn of worship? When I'm on my deathbed, can the last beat of my heart be a hymn of love celebrating Your unmatched grace?

2. Lord Jesus, I come before You just to worship, adore and exalt Your wonderful name, the name that is above all names. You are the King of kings, Lord of

lords, Prince of Peace, Unchangeable Changer, and Mighty Man in battle, the Beginning and the End. I glorify Your holy name forever more.

3. Jesus, You are the Way, the Truth and the Life. Heaven and Earth adore You and angels bow before You. You are beautiful, awesome, wonderful and glorious. I worship You and I praise Your holy name forever more.

4. Oh Christ, You are the Bread of Life, my Great Provider, faithful and True Witness, the Captain and Commander-in-Chief of the armies of Heaven.

5. Lord Jesus, You are the Opener of hearts, the powerful King, the one who raises the dead, the God of all hope. You are the one who delivered us from eternal death and showed us the way to the Father. There is none like You; You are good, kind, and full of mercy.

6. Lord Jesus, it is only because of Your unfailing love and grace and because of Your unconditional love that we can even consider coming into Your presence. It is through Your sacrifice that we are able to approach the throne of grace to obtain mercy; I worship and glorify You, Lord Jesus.

7. Lord Jesus, You are worthy, You are wonderful, You are more than what we could ever ask or image. I will praise You, Lord, with all my heart; I will tell of all the wonderful and glorious things You have done.

8. You are Emmanuel, God with us, Good Teacher, my Shepherd, Messiah, the Resurrection and the Life, the

Author of Eternal salvation, the Ransom, Lamb without blemish, the Lamb of God, the Holy One of Israel! You are Holy and unchanging. Lord, You are the Savior of the world.

9.  You are the Great Shepherd of Israel, the Light of the world, the Maker of all things, the First Born among many brethren.

10. You alone deserve all the glory, honor, power, authority, dominion, majesty and all Excellencies forever and ever. Amen.

## The Names and Titles of Jesus

| | |
|---|---|
| Revelation 1:8 | Alpha and Omega |
| Revelation 2:28 | Bright Morning Star |
| Revelation 5:5 | Lion of the Tribe of Judah |
| Revelation 17:14 | Lord of lords and King of kings |
| Romans 11:26 | Deliverer |
| Daniel 7:13-14 | Ancient of Days |
| Isaiah 9:6 | Prince of Peace |
| Jeremiah 8:22 | Balm of Gilead |
| John 6:35 | Bread of Life |
| Song of Solomon 5:10 | Fairest among of Ten Thousand |
| Song of Solomon 2:1 | Rose of Sharon |
| Song of Solomon 2:1 | Lilly of the Valleys |

| | |
|---|---|
| Isaiah 9:6 | Wonderful, Counselor |
| Revelation 3:14 | Faithful and True Witness |
| Roman 8:29 | Firstborn among many brethren |
| Hebrews 12:2 | Finisher of our faith |
| Proverbs 18:24 | Friend who sticks closer than a brother |
| Matthew 1:23 | Immanuel – God with us |
| John 1:29 | Lamb of God |
| 1 Peter 1:19 | Lamb without blemish |
| Isaiah 43:14 | Lord Your Redeemer |
| John 11:23 | Resurrection and the Life |
| Mark 10:45 | The Ransom |

# WORSHIP GOD THE HOLY SPIRIT OF THE LORD

### *Corinthians 3:17*
### *Now the Lord is the Spirit; and where the Spirit of the Lord is, there is liberty.*

1. Blessed Holy Spirit, I want to thank You for Your work and ministry in my life.
2. What can I do without You, my dear Friend and Companion, my Teacher and Counselor, my Advocate and Guide?
3. You are the Holy Guest, the Special Guest who we entertain.
4. I just want to tell You I love You, I need You and I want You. To You alone, my spirit yields.
5. You are the Spirit of Truth, the Spirit of Life, the Spirit of Power, and the Spirit of Wisdom.
6. I thank You for all that You are doing for me and through me. I yield my whole life to You. Take me, break me, mold me, and use me.
7. You are the immortal and invisible Spirit of God, the gentle and immaculate Dove from Heaven, the Sweet Wind that brings life and refreshing from the throne of God.

8. The Enabler of the saints, the indwelling Presence, O sweet Spirit of the Living God, come and fill us to overflowing with Your love and power.

9. Sovereign Spirit of God, come, overshadow and brood over me, as the hen broods over her eggs. Activate Your gifts and fruits in my life. Let the fire of Pentecost fall afresh on me.

10. Quicken and energize my mortal body, strengthen my inner man, O gracious Spirit of God.

11. Holy Ghost, You are the number one weapon for spiritual warfare. You are a consuming fire who will lead me gently to my attacker. Consume whatever is oppressing, depressing and suppressing me in Jesus' name.

12. My restoration and deliverance have come through the power of the Holy Spirit.

13. Let the winds of the Holy Spirit blow upon me with great dominion in Jesus' name.

14. Saturate and permeate every fiber of my being with Your holy anointing. Incubate and clothe me with the glory of God.

15. Let thy dew from Heaven fall upon my thirsty soul, O sweet Spirit of God. Come and take control of my life.

16. Fill my cup until I want no more. Anoint my head with oil. Cause my cup to run over.

17. Eternal Spirit of the living God, thank You once again for all the wonderful things You are doing in my life.

# ADORATION OF GOD, THE HOLY SPIRIT

Holy Spirit is God, a person. He is not energy or a force, just as much as the other two members of the trinity.

- Holy Spirit is God.
- He is treated on an equal basis with God, the Father and God, the Son.
- He has the characteristics of God.
- He does the work of God.

Holy Spirit, it is You who makes me see everything. It is You who's shown me the way to realize my ideals. It is You who gave me the Godly gift of forgiveness, allowing me to forgive all that has been done to me. It is You who is in every area of my life. I want to thank You for everything and confirm once again with You that I never want to part with You, no matter what material desires I have. I want to be with You and my loved ones in Your eternal glory. Amen.

1. Holy Spirit, You are our Advocate, our Helper, and the Source of our power. We respect and honor You, the Triune God.
2. Sweet Spirit of the living God, I accept You as the Dispenser of my life. You are the power that is working within us. May You rule over my eternity. I adore You, I praise You, and I worship You.
3. Holy Spirit of God who helps me to bear witness and

testify of Jesus, You are the Great Teacher and Master of all hidden things. You are holy, awesome, glorious, and powerful. I worship and adore You. I love You.

4. You are the Spirit of Truth, the Spirit of Life, the Spirit of Power, and the Spirit of Wisdom.

5. You are the immortal and invisible Spirit of God, the gentle and immaculate Dove from Heaven, the Sweet Wind that brings life and refreshing from the throne of God.

6. Holy Ghost, You are the number one weapon for spiritual warfare. You are a consuming fire who will lead me gently past my attacker. Consume whatever is oppressing, depressing and suppressing me, in Jesus' name.

7. Holy Spirit of the living God, my perpetual Succor who lives with me, never to leave me. I adore and glorify You.

8. Holy Spirit of God who makes me aware of my sins and iniquities, and always helps me to turn to God, I worship You and I will love You forever.

## SCRIPTURAL REFERENCES

| | |
|---|---|
| Isaiah 11:2 | Our Counselor |
| Zechariah 12:10 | Spirit of Grace |
| John 14:16 | Our Helper |
| John 14:17 | Spirit of Truth |
| John 14:26 | Our Teacher |

| | |
|---|---|
| John 15:26 | Our Comforter |
| John 16:13 | Our Guide |
| Luke 24:49 | The Spirit of Promise |
| Acts 1:8 | The Spirit of Power |
| 2 Corinthians 3:6 | The Spirit of Life |
| 2 Corinthians 3:17 | The Spirit of Liberty |

# JESUS: HIS REALITY, RELATIONSHIPS AND REWARDS

1. Jesus, You are the light. Cause Your light to shine on every dark area of my life. Shine in my darkness, and let darkness never comprehend nor overtake me again. In Your precious name.
2. Lord Jesus, You are my Salvation from every situation of bondage. Save me today. I ask in Your precious name.
3. Lord Jesus, You are my Jubilee. Break every yoke in my life, and cause joy and jubilation to be the song of my life. In Your precious name. Amen.
4. Lord Jesus, You are the Star out of Jacob, my anti-curse and my Shield from the enemy. Break every curse operating in my life, in Jesus' name (Numbers 24:17).
5. Lord Jesus, You are my blessing. Qualify me and enable me to receive the prophetic blessing of Deuteronomy 33, in Your precious name.
6. Lord Jesus, You are the Captain of the Host of the Lord. Come into every battle raging in my life and guarantee victory, in Your precious name.
7. Lord Jesus, You are the Source of my great strength. Continue to strengthen me to do Your will and Your work forever.
8. Lord Jesus, You are my cover and my nearest kinsman.

Cover me and let Your blood keep flowing in my veins.

9. Lord Jesus, You are the spoken Word of God that called Samuel to serve God. Speak to me clearly and let me understand my divine assignment.

10. My Savior and my Lord, You are the move of God. Continue to move on my behalf in every area of my life.

11. Lord, You are the Wisdom of God and the Lion of Judah. You destroy the disobedient and guard the humble. Deliver me from disobedience and give me humility in serving You.

12. Lord Jesus, You are the manifestation of miracles and the one who gives life beyond the grave. Bring me out of all of my grief with Your revival power.

13. Lord Jesus, what You bless becomes blessed forever. You love Your own, and You love them until the end. Bless me with Your everlasting blessing and love me until the end as Your own.

14. Lord, You are the God of abundance and power, and You show Yourself strong on behalf of Your own. Please perfect my heart and show Yourself strong in my life.

15. You are the Lord of remembrance and restoration. Remind me of Your will that I have forgotten and restore to me everything that I have lost, in Your precious name.

16. You are the Lord of favor and vengeance. Bless me with the favor of Esther and let my Haman hang in his own gallows.

17. Lord Jesus, You can do everything, and no thought can be withheld from You. Do everything necessary in my life for me to possess my prepared places and fulfill my destiny.

18. You are the only begotten Son of God. The uttermost parts of the Earth are in Your possession. Make me globally effective for Your Kingdom.

19. Lord, You are Wonderful, Counselor, Mighty God, Everlasting Father, Prince of Peace, Emmanuel and the Lamb of God. Let Your wonder work in my life. Let Your counsel stand in my life. Place Your might between me and every enemy of my life, for You are my everlasting Father.

20. Lord Jesus, You sanctified and ordained us as prophets to the nations. Sanctify me and empower me to proclaim Your prophetic word to the nations.

21. Manifest Your greatness in all areas of my life.

22. Lord Jesus, You are the Dayspring from on high. Visit my life and grant me a positive new beginning and the next wave of Your glory.

23. Lord Jesus, make Your rewards manifest positively in every area of my life. In Your mighty, everlasting name I pray, Amen!

# PRAYERS FOR THE ANOINTING

*Isaiah 10:27*
*It shall come to pass in that day That his burden will be taken away from your shoulder, And his yoke from your neck, And the yoke will be destroyed because of the anointing oil.*

1. Lord, let Your Spirit come upon me. Anoint me with the power of Your Holy Spirit, and let me experience light, revelation, insight, and clarified vision.
2. Let Your anointing provide spice and fragrance for my life.
3. Lord, deliver my head from every contamination and cleanse it from every negative anointing.
4. Father, let Your anointing cause the fragrance of blessedness to ooze out of my life.
5. Father God, let Your anointing consecrate me and make me supernatural, extraordinary, and uniquely dedicated to You.
6. Let me be so full of the power of Your anointing that everything about me will be anointed. Anoint my garments, my borders, my furniture and all I touch! Let Your anointing upon my life consecrate everything I come in contact with.
7. Let Your anointing upon my life be so pure that my carnality cannot contaminate me.

8. Let my utterances be full of Your power, and let my ministry be connected to Your power.

9. Let Your anointing grant me the power to get wealth, a powrer that makes me rich without adding sorrow to it.

10. May Your anointing manifest in my life by convicting and converting sinners to become saints.

11. May Your anointing in me purify lives that have been defiled by sin, and purify those souls in Jesus' name.

12. Lord, let Your anointing upon my life go by Your grace from generation to generation to the glory of Your holy name.

13. Give me the grace to be Kingdom-minded and to be a responsible minister all the days of my life.

14. Lord, let me be able to eat and drink with great joy in Your presence; let me not be ashamed of manifesting gladness in Your presence.

15. Father God, let Your anointing break every yoke in my life and set me free to be who You have purposed me to be in my generation.

16. Lord, let Your anointing heal me and all whom I minister to, in Jesus' name.

17. Let Your anointing light the fire of the Holy Spirit in my life, and make me a minister who is a flame of fire, untouchable by evil and every cold hand of destruction that is formed against me.

18. Let the anointing that I have received from You, O Lord, abide in me and teach me all things.

19. Let Your anointing give me the grace to always abide in You. In Jesus' name I pray.

# PRAYERS FOR THE NATION

*II Chronicles 7:14*
*If My people who are called by My name will humble themselves, and pray and seek My face, and turn from their wicked ways, then I will hear from heaven, and will forgive their sin and heal their land.*

1. Almighty God, I come before You, in the name of Jesus, to intercede for this great nation and its people.
2. First, I want to thank You for our nation and its Godly heritage, for our founding fathers were known to be men who loved and feared God. All that we are and have, we owe to Your loving grace.
3. Lord, I confess the sins of the people of this land before You. We have sinned and have done wickedly. Have mercy on us, O God. Hear our confession and pardon our iniquities. Restore to us the former glory which we are losing as a result of our sins.
4. Sprinkle the blood of Your Son, Jesus, over this land and over our people, and sanctify us unto Yourself. Draw us as a nation to Your side by the power of Your Spirit.
5. Turn away Your anger from this land, and restrain the remainder of Your wrath. For You are our Defense, our Strong Tower and our Hiding place. You are our God, and in You, we trust.

6. By Your grace, O Lord, I build up the wall and stand in the gap before You for our land so that this land might be spared from eternal destruction, in Jesus' name.

7. Overthrow ungodly leaders and raise up leaders who are filled with Your Spirit. Save and guide the leaders of our government on all levels.

8. Establish excellence in our educational system, integrity in our news media, righteous judgment in our courts, fairness and justice in our law enforcement agencies, honesty and truth in our government. You are the Almighty God who can overthrow the mighty.

9. Father, in the name of Jesus, I come against the strongholds of the devil in this nation, and I pull them down.

10. Father, in the name of Jesus, I break the power of demonic influences that have risen in our land. I bind every demonic power of pride, compromise, false authority, witchcraft, false signs and wonders, oppression, bondage, deceit, idolatry, and every radical demonic spirit in Jesus' name.

11. I lift the name of Jesus against the lying spirit of the occult, witchcraft, Satanism, paganism, and all false religions. I render their powers powerless, in Jesus' name.

12. God, pull back the covers and expose the enemy in hidden dark places.

13. Expose their deception with Your truth, O God, and free their victims.

14. I plead the blood of Jesus against the filthy spirits of immorality and sodomy that possesses great numbers of men and women in this land, and cast them out in Jesus' name.

15. I put a clog in the wheel of the pornographic industries. Save the souls of the owners and operators of this immoral enterprise.

16. I bind the destructive spirits of greed, lawlessness, violence, prejudice, terror, and rebellion, and I cast them down to the bottomless pit. I render their powers over their victims powerless, in the name of Jesus.

17. I curse the soil that produces cocaine, heroine, and all other mind-altering and life-destroying substances. May it be subdued in Jesus' name. I command that soil to become barren and yield nothing.

18. Lord Jesus, You cursed a fig tree and it withered. I curse every drug plantation, and command it to wither after the order of the fig tree, in Jesus' name.

19. Lord, our sins are ever great before You, and it's a stench to Your nostrils. Our sins of godlessness, pride, materialism, truth-breaking, identity crisis, prejudice, racism, terror, rebellion, all kinds of addictions, divorce, gambling, economic debt, ungodly trash on the television and social media, innocent blood-shed, abortion, involvement in the occult, involvement in outright satanic worship, lack of compassion for the poor, the abandonment of our children to the evils of worldly peer pressures, false families, domestic

violence, and wickedness of every kind have separated us from the True and Living God.

20. Bless this land again with abundant prosperity. Heal our homes and unite our families. Sweeten relationships between family members, neighbors, and our fellow citizens.

21. May our homes be filled with dancing and our streets be filled with joy.

22. Almighty God, abort every terrorist plan. Expose their plans and hiding places. Frustrate and thwart every one of their activities, inside and outside our borders.

23. Lord, watch over our land, and let not the weapons of hatred and wickedness take the life of any of our citizens.

24. Safety is of the Lord. You are our Defense and Shield. Bring upon us an absolute sense of safety and security.

25. I pray for a great outpouring and visitation of Your Spirit all across this land.

26. Lord, reveal the hiding agenda to Your servants, the prophets.

27. As promised through Your prophet Joel, pour out Your Spirit upon our sons and daughters, upon our old men and women. Revive us again, O God.

28. Now to the King eternal, immortal, invisible, the only true and wise God, be honor, power, and glory forever and ever. Amen.

## SCRIPTURAL REFERENCES

| | |
|---|---|
| Psalm 33:12 | Blessed is the nation whose God is the Lord; and the people whom he hath chosen for his own inheritance. |
| Prov 14:34 | Righteousness exalts a nation, but sin is a reproach to any people. |
| Psalm 9:17 | The wicked shall be turn into hell, and all the nations that forget God. |
| Ezekiel 22:30 | So I sought for a man among them who would make a wall, and stand in the gap before Me on behalf of the land, that I should not destroy it; but I found no one. |
| Isaiah 60:18 | Violence shall no longer be heard in Your land, neither wasting nor destruction within Your borders. |

# Intercession for Political and Government Leaders

*1 Timothy 2:1*
*Therefore I exhort first of all that supplications, prayers, intercessions, and giving of thanks be made for all men, 2 for kings and all who are in authority, that we may lead a quiet and peaceable life in all godliness and reverence.*

1. Father in Heaven, I come to intercede for the political leaders of this nation and the nations of the world.
2. Lord, raise up leaders like David, Your servant, a man after Your own heart, a man filled with Your Spirit and anointed with Your holy oil.
3. Guide the affairs of our nation through the hands of our President and leaders. Give them wisdom like Solomon, and give them a sincere love and concern for humanity.
4. Cause them to make laws that protect the freedom, equality and liberty of all citizens.
5. May they formulate policies, both domestic and foreign, that harmonize the peaceful co-existence of all men in this nation and the world as a global community.
6. Help to settle political differences with peaceful solutions. Let diplomacy prevail in international conflicts and threats, instead of war and destruction.

7. Overthrow evil leaders, brutal dictators, and oppressive regimes who are demonically instigated and controlled by the devil. Remove them from the corridor of power.

8. Expose and remove from office all corrupt and immoral leaders.

9. Guide our political processes, safeguard our democracy and elections, and rid our nation of fraud, greed, desensitization to sin, and corruption. May the choice and mandate of the people and God prevail in all elections.

10. Lord, restrain political assassinations and stop politics of bitterness and rancor. Teach our aspiring leaders civility, and help them to learn how to take defeat with dignity.

11. Lord, put Your fear in the hearts of all electoral officials that they may conduct free and fair elections.

12. Choose great men of integrity, transparency, honesty, and a great sense of justice to oversee and referee our electoral process. Choose men who will abhor bribery, men who cannot be bought with money or influences.

13. Father, I pray for a Godly Deborah, God's agent of justice and truth on Earth who, not only dispenses righteous judgments and justice, but is also a prophetic messenger, revealing Your nature, purpose and will to the nations. Raise up Deborahs to stand in the gap, even at their own personal risk and danger, women who will intercede until victory is achieved. Is

anything too difficult for God? Nothing shall be impossible for You, O Lord.

14. Lord, it was You who touched, used and even transformed hearts of kings and rulers throughout history—from Pharaoh to Abimelech to Nebuchadnezzar. It was You, Lord, who intervened in the lives of our political leaders—the ones who changed history and served Your purpose.

15. Father, may Your Kingdom come, may Your will be done in this land. Amen.

# INTERCESSION FOR SPIRITUAL LEADERS

*Ephesians 6:18*
*Praying always with all prayer and supplication in the Spirit, being watchful to this end with all perseverance and supplication for all the saints— and for me, that utterance may be given to me, that I may open my mouth boldly to make known the mystery of the gospel.*

1. Most High God, I humbly approach Your throne now to intercede for Your servants, the leaders and overseers of Your church in this country and all over the world.

2. Lord, anoint these leaders with a mighty anointing. Enrich their preaching and teaching with great power, grace, and fruitfulness, leading to the conversion of sinners. Bless their social media platforms, bless the works of their hands, and bless their labor, in the name of Jesus.

3. Lord, cause them to see and experience a greater move of Your Spirit, greater miracles, signs, and wonders, greater revelation, greater conviction, greater conversion, and greater deliverance to the praise and glory of Your name.

4. Protect them from the tongue of liars and haters of God. Shield them from the mocking and the attack of

38

social media trolls.

5. Lord, strike the persecutors of Your servants, Yourambassadors, Your beloved and Your church (which is the Body of Christ) down from their high-horses of pride and arrogance with Your mighty hand as You did with Saul of Tarsus, and make them preachers of the gospel and lovers of Jesus Christ.

6. Let the Great Light from Heaven encompass these persecutors, and let the voice of Majesty speak and rebuke their persecuting. "Thus saith the Lord God, It shall not stand, neither shall it come to pass," according to Isaiah 7:7.

7. Lord, send these leaders as You did Peter to the Cornelius in the inner cities who are thirsty and hungry for the Word of God, the Gospel of the Lord, Jesus Christ, and also to the nations where the doors have been shut to the gospel and to their social media platforms.

8. Make them strong for Yourself. Keep them from falling. Keep them from error. Let the spirits of Jezebel, greed and covetousness never have dominion over them.

9. Release a deeper encounter with You that will position our spiritual leaders for the new move of the Spirit that is upon the Church and social media.

10. Lord, You are calling them out into the place of the greatest awakening of their lives concerning their destinies and the plans that You have for them.

11. Lord, rekindle in them a burning desire, a fresh vision, an overwhelming zeal, and an intense passion for the things of Your Kingdom.

12. Father, grant our spiritual leaders great wisdom like that of Solomon, to walk in meekness like Moses. Cause them to walk in integrity, holiness and truth. Grant them favor with kings, princes, and with all men.

13. Disarm principalities and powers of evil that are on assignment against their lives, ministries, and families.

14. Thwart and frustrate all of their plans and activities against Your anointed ones, O God, our Redeemer.

15. Father, come upon Your ambassadors like a fresh and brisk wind, and fill them up to overflowing with a fresh anointing.

16. Let Your angels pursue warlocks and evil agents, and let them disarm them whenever they are gathered against Your servants.

17. Send Your angels as their bodyguards to protect and keep them from harm's way.

All of these prayers I offer to You, in the precious name of Jesus. Amen.

# INTERCESSION FOR THE CITY

***Psalm 127:1***
***Unless the Lord builds the house, they labor in vain who build it; unless the Lord guards the city, The watchman stays awake in vain.***

1. Father, I come before You now to intercede for this great city and its surroundings.
2. Lord, save the leaders and workers of the city government, businesses, educational institutions, news media, social media, landmarks, law enforcement agencies, security checkpoints, supermarkets, hospitals, retail establishments, entertainment and all other service industries.
3. God, stir up the people of this city and its surroundings. Arouse us to a great spiritual awakening. Draw the hearts of the careless and the godless to seek for mercy. Draw communities to unite in prayer and revival. I prophesy that the scent of revival will be in this city, in Jesus' name.
4. I send up an exceedingly great and sorrowful cry to You on behalf of the multitude who do not know You in this city. Open their hearts to the true gospel. Let the gospel spread abroad and reach the hearts in our communities like never before, in Jesus' name.
5. My earnest prayers go up to Your throne now for sinners, for men and women, boys and girls who are

polluted and ravaged by sins in this city. Bring many to Christ's feet; draw them with Your irresistible power.

6. With great compassion, stretch forth Your long arm, Your mighty arm, and pull them out of the sewer of sin, and wash them clean in the fountain of the blood of Jesus. Convert multitudes and cause them to flock to Christ with weeping and repentant hearts.

7. Great and Mighty God, there is nothing too hard for You. Save and deliver multitudes who are still wallowing in drugs, alcohol, rage, immorality, false families, witchcraft and other evil practices, and make them great lovers of Christ Jesus.

8. Lord, I pray that You stop the numerous sinful activities that are everywhere on our street corners.

9. Let Your eternal power and glory flood our cities as the water covers the sea. Let Your divine presence fill and saturate the atmosphere over our cities, our homes, schools, hospitals, supermarkets, retail establishments, offices and our churches, as well as our social media platforms.

10. Stop teenage pregnancy, juvenile delinquency, rebellion and everything that is destroying a great number of our young people who are our hope of tomorrow.

11. Send upon this city and its inhabitants great revival, seasons of great spiritual refreshing, and great outpouring of Your Spirit.

12. Cause gang violence, pedophilia, bloodshed, armed robbery, drug trafficking, and sex trafficking to cease,

and the perpetrators to lay down their weapons of violence and hatred. Draw them by Your power to the cross of Christ Jesus.

13. Remove drug trafficking from our streets and sex trafficking from our cities and neighborhoods. Watch over our cities. Send Your angels to patrol our streets and restrain crimes.

14. Let those the Father gave to Christ be brought out from among the people of this city into His church.

15. Chase the demon-in-charge of this city and his demonic host out into the bottomless pit.

16. I come against the strongholds of religious spirits and false doctrines in this city. I pull them down and destroy them to the very foundation, in Jesus' name.

17. Have mercy on all who are poor and homeless in this city. Bless and prosper them greatly.

18. Remember the prisoners and inmates who have no helper. Comfort them with Your love, and speed up their release and freedom. Raise a banner of Christ's freedom in their souls. Above all, save their souls.

19. Great Physician from Galilee, visit those who are on their sick beds, in nursing homes, and in hospice care, emergency rooms and ICU. Heal and make them well speedily. Bring back to life those who are dying, if it be Your will, in Jesus' name.

20. Prosper the good businesses in this city so that many who are out of employment may have jobs. I make a prophetic declaration that there is no unemployment

in the Kingdom. I am to be about my Father's business.

21. Bless all work done for You in this city. Bless Your children, especially those of the household of faith. May we never lack resources to do what You have called us to do in this city.

I know whatsoever I ask in prayer, believing, I will receive. I receive the answers to these prayers now, in Jesus' name. Amen.

| SCRIPTURAL REFERENCES | |
|---|---|
| 1 Timothy 2:1 | Therefore I exhort first of all that supplications, prayers, intercessions, and giving of thanks be made for all men, for kings and all who are in authority, that we may lead a quiet and peaceable life in all godliness and reverence. |
| Job 16:21 | Oh, that one might plead for a man with God, As a man pleads for his neighbor! |

# INTERCESSION FOR JERUSALEM

### *Psalm 122:6*
### *Pray for the peace of Jerusalem, they shall prosper that love You.*

1. Great and Awesome God, I come before Your throne to intercede for the city of David, Your servant, and for the inhabitants of Jerusalem, Your holy city.
2. Lord, I stand in the gap between You and Your people. I plead for mercy on their behalf. I confess the sins of Your people before You and ask for Your pardon.
3. I pray for the peace of Jerusalem, for peace to reign within its borders, and prosperity within its cities.
4. Our God, open Your ear and hear the disastrous sound of suicide bombings, health hazards, and every evil plot to destroy mankind. Open Your eyes and see the destruction of lives and properties in Your holy city!
5. Lord, listen! O Lord, hear! O Lord, see! And act speedily. Put an end to these acts of violence and destruction against Your chosen ones, the children and descendants of Your friend, Abraham.
6. Remember Your covenant with Your friend, Abraham, and make peace between his two descendants Isaac and Ishmael for Your name and glory's sake.
7. Help bring a peaceful and acceptable compromise in the interest of both sides, for You are Father of them

all.

8. Cause these two sworn enemies to become loving neighbors that they might dwell side by side in peace and harmony, for You are God, and there is nothing too hard for You.

9. Let it not be said concerning our God that He is weak or does not care about the plight of His own people, seeing that Your own very people dwell in constant conflict, fear, and insecurity.

10. I pray for the leaders of Israel, and I ask that You guide and direct the affairs of the state of Israel by their hands, as You did with David, Your servant.

11. Remember Your word in Isaiah 32:18, where You promised Your people, saying, "My people will dwell in a peaceful habitation, in secure dwellings, and in quiet resting places." Bring this promise to pass, O God, our Father!

12. Lord, I pray that there will be such a peace in Israel so that the children may play again on the streets of Jerusalem without fear of terror, and that Your people might live, move freely, and dwell in safety in the holy city of our God.

13. God of Abraham, Isaac and Jacob, I ask these things and much more to be done for Your people, in Jesus' name. Amen.

## SCRIPTURAL REFERENCES

| | |
|---|---|
| Psalm 122:7-9 | Peace be within Your walls, prosperity within Your palaces." For the sake of my brethren and companions, I will now say, "Peace be within you." Because of the house of the Lord, our God I will seek Your good. |
| Psalm 137:5-6 | If I forget you, O Jerusalem, Let my right hand forget its skill! If I do not remember you, let my tongue cling to the roof of my mouth—If I do not exalt Jerusalem above my chief joy. |
| Psalm 137:7 | Remember, O Lord, against the sons of Edom the day of Jerusalem, who said, "Raze it, raze it, to its very foundation!" O daughter of Babylon, who are to be destroyed, Happy the one who repays you as you have served us! |
| Isaiah 32:18 | My people will dwell in a peaceful habitation, in secure dwellings, and in quiet resting places. |
| Isaiah 60:18 | Violence shall no longer be heard in your land, Neither wasting nor destruction within your borders. |
| Isaiah 62:1 | For Zion's sake I will not hold My peace, And for Jerusalem's sake I will not rest, Until her righteousness goes forth as |

| | |
|---|---|
| | brightness, And her salvation as a lamp that burns. |
| Genesis 12:3 | I will bless those who bless you, and I will curse him who curses you; And in you all the families of the Earth shall be blessed. |
| Zechariah 2:8 | For this is what the Lord Almighty says: "After he has honoured me and has sent me against the nations that have plundered you—for whoever touches you touches the apple of his eye. |
| Ezekiel 16:24 | For I will take you from among the nations, gather you out of all countries, and bring you into your own land. |
| 1 Samuel 12:23 | God forbid that I should sin against the Lord in ceasing to pray for You. |
| Psalm 51:18 | Do good in Your good pleasure to Zion; build the walls of Jerusalem. |

# INTERCESSION FOR THE CHURCH AND SOCIAL MEDIA PLATFORMS

***Matthew 16:18***
***And I also say to You that You are Peter, and on this rock I will build My church, and the gates of hell shall not prevail against it.***

1. Heavenly Father, I come boldly to Your throne, to plead for Your Church. May Your ears be open and attentive to my pleas.
2. Bless Your church and all the works that are done in Your name around the world.
3. There's a shift from Church to Kingdom, and King Jesus will rule over all. Saul is dead! The old wineskin, religious order is over.
4. The Church is breaking through and coming to a new level, a reset, an apostolic order, a new era and a divine alignment, in the name of Jesus!
5. The New Wine is in the cluster, the Church and social media will rise up, bounce back, embrace the move of the Holy Spirit, and walk in Kingdom brotherhood.
6. Shepherd of Israel, deal a heavy blow to the wolves. Drive them out of the midst of Your Sheep. "My sheep hear my voice, and I know them, and they follow me" (John 10:27).
7. I come against the spirit of Jezebel, which perpetrates

immorality in the Church of Christ, and even on social media platforms. I bind you, spirit of Jezebel, and cast you to the pit, in Jesus' name.

8. I bind the devil and every demon on assignment against my assignment for ministry.

9. God, You are coming back for a Church without a spot or a wrinkle.

10. Make a pathway of ministry, responsibility and integrity for me, and make me a treasurer of Kingdom resources for ministry.

11. Let me stand before kings and not before mere men. Make me known in Your Presence and unknown before their presence.

12. Lord, there's a mighty move of Your Spirit upon the Church and social media where integrity and holiness will be seen like never before.

# PRAYERS FOR THE NEW WINE

1. O Father God, I thank You for Your awesome presence, and where Your presence is, new wine begins to flow. You are manufacturing new wine as I seek You and engross in Your presence. The wineskin must be made new. Behold, You are doing a new thing that will dismantle the old.

2. Lord, You are dismantling the walls of strongholds, bitterness, unforgiveness, fear, offense, coldheartedness, and rejection. You are ripping down, pulling up, tearing up and throwing away the old, and You are rebuilding the new. "And no man putteth new wine into old bottles: else the new wine doth burst the bottles, and the wine is spilled, and the bottles will be marred: but new wine must be put into new bottles" (Mark 2:22).

3. The trap that has been set for me by the enemy is broken.

4. The trap that the enemy has set for me through distraction, fear, torment and confusion is broken.

5. I decree that I shall move into this new wineskin with greater ease.

6. I thank You for the new wine and Your glory that's been poured out and displayed in my life.

7. I am going from the winepress to victory, in Jesus' name.                                    Amen.

# INTERCESSION FOR REVIVAL AND REFORMATION

*Ephesians 2:20*
*Built on the foundation of the apostles and prophets, with Christ Jesus Himself as the cornerstone.*

1.  Father God, in the name of Jesus, I am a worshiper, and I have the fear of God, and not men.
2.  Heavenly Father, I thank You for Your calling upon my life. Thank You for making me an able minister of the gospel of the Lord, Jesus Christ. Psalms 104:4 says, "Who makes His angels spirits, His ministers a flaming fire."
3.  Uphold and uplift my being, my standing, and my voice in this end-time movement.
4.  Lord, anoint me with a double portion of Your Spirit. Empower me to teach and preach with divine unction and boldness.
5.  I thank You that I am a living echo of Your voice—I am a word in season from You to the discouraged saints in their needful hour.
6.  What I recognize, I energize. You are leading me so that I may lead wandering and wavering feet into Your power and glory.
7.  Let Your burden-removing, yoke-destroying, curse-breaking, spell-annulling, and devil-casting anointing

rest upon me without measure, as it was on Jesus.

8. Impart unto me the nine spiritual gifts: faith, power, word of knowledge, word of wisdom, prophecy, tongues and interpretation of tongues, discerning of spirits, and working of miracles so that they may be made manifest in my life and ministry for the edification and equipping of the saints.

9. I thank You for feeding me that I may feed Your hungry sons and daughters with manna straight from Heaven.

10. Lord, I thank You for using me as a conduit for the outflow of Your divine power to heal the sick, raise the dead, open the eyes of the blind, open the ears of the deaf, make the lame walk, cause the dumb to speak, and to cleanse the lepers.

11. The fear of the Lord is the beginning of wisdom and knowledge.

12. I submit to the Lord of Hosts and Five-Fold ministry gifts, and live a disciplined life unto the Lord Jesus.

13. Lord, I thank You for purifying my heart so I can see You.

14. I am a leader of integrity, called and anointed by God, and sent by the Lord. I bind the spirit of Saul.

15. I take the sword of the Spirit of God, and I sever the cords of domination, intimidation, and manipulation, in Jesus' name and through the blood of the Lamb!

16. I cast out the spirit of drunkenness, lies, backbiting, gossip, witchcraft, and all works of iniquity, in Jesus' name.

17. I give my all to Jesus Christ, and I dethrone the works of the flesh, the exalting of man and I convict the proud flesh.

18. I pull down religious and political powers in the realm of the spirit over the church and social media.

19. I am a habitation for the Lord.

20. There is no compromise in the Word of God.

21. I am bold to confront sin. Let the wind of the Holy Spirit blow through social media, churches, and ministries, and cleanse everything unholy.

22. I bind hypocrisy, and I release transparency and humility in the hearts of believers.

23. Father in Heaven, strengthen me so that while I stand firm on the Rock and strong in faith, I may stretch out a loving hand to the perishing souls and rescue them from the flames of hell.

24. Father, thank You for a fresh anointing, and for preaching and teaching with all clarity, revelation, comfort, and convicting power.

25. Give me the tongue of the learned.

26. Send us times of revival, and send us the season of great refreshing, and the outpouring of Your Spirit.

27. Maximize Your anointing, all spiritual gifts, fruits, talents, and potential that You have put inside of me.

28. I have come to the Kingdom for such a time as this to gather together and stand for the Kingdom of God and for our lives to destroy, to slay, and to cause to perish all the powers that assault and terrorize us, and

to spoil these powers of their prey, in the Almighty
name of Jesus.

## SCRIPTURAL REFERENCES

| 2 Corinthians 3:6 | Who also made us sufficient as ministers of the new covenant, not of the letter but of the Spirit; for the letter kills, but the Spirit gives life. |
|---|---|
| Ephesians 3:7 | Of which I became a minister according to the gift of the grace of God given to me by the effective working of His power. |
| John 21:17 | He said to him the third time, "Simon, son of Jonah, do you love Me?" Peter was grieved because He said to him the third time, "Do you love Me?" And he said to Him, "Lord, You know all things; You know that I love You." Jesus said to him, "Feed My sheep. |
| Acts 26:16 - 18 | But rise and stand on your feet; for I have appeared to you for this purpose, to make you a minister and a witness both of the things which you have seen and of the things which I will yet reveal to you. I will deliver you from the Jewish people, as well as from the Gentiles, to whom I now send you, to open their eyes, in order to turn them from darkness to light, and from the power of Satan to God, that they may |

| | |
|---|---|
| | receive forgiveness of sins and an inheritance among those who are sanctified by faith in Me.' |
| Matthew 10:7-8 | And as you go, preach, saying, 'The Kingdom of Heaven is at hand.' Heal the sick, cleanse the lepers, raise the dead, cast out demons. Freely you have received, freely give. |

# PRAYERS AGAINST JEZEBEL

1. Foul spirit of Jezebel, I render your powers of control and death powerless, in Jesus' name. I stand against you, in Jesus' name! It is written in the Word of God that whatsoever I bind on Earth shall be bound in Heaven, and whatsoever I loose on Earth shall be loosed in Heaven. So, I bind up the spirit of Jezebel in the heavenlies. I bind up Jezebel with chains from Heaven, and I loose God's holy warring angels to battle on our behalf.

2. I take authority and break every witchcraft spirit, every faultfinder spirit, and all spirits of slander, scandal, defamation, accusations, all spirits of Jezebel, every eavesdropper spirit, every jealous spirit, spirits of persecution, prosecution, opposition, hindrance, interference, and obstruction, and all blocking spirits, spirits of confusion, division, lies, discord, distraction, character assassination, fear , depression, and every foul spirit, in the name of Jesus.

3. I bind the spirit of death, and I break soul ties, old ties, and old fragments between Jezebel and her children.

4. I bind unforgiveness, guilt, rejection, evil reports, gossip, demonic whispering, criticism, pain, fear, double-mindedness, headaches, witchcraft, insanity, compromise, and sympathy.

5. I break the spirits of the false judge, the false accuser, the false comforter, and the false advocate, in the Almighty name of Jesus.

6. I bind Jezebel's efforts to destroy families. I declare the hearts of the fathers and mothers will return to their children, and the hearts of the children to their parents.

7. I break the spirit of passive aggressive behaviors, and I put division between Jezebel and her husband, Ahab and Pharaoh, in the mighty name of Jesus. You are defeated and your men are destroyed.

8. I take away and destroy all false idols, adultery, fornication, identity crisis, and all sacrifices destroying the sanctity of marriage, in the name of Jesus. I release submission, unity and commitment! The two shall become one flesh.

9. I rebuke all spirits of false teaching and prophecy connected to Jezebel, in Jesus' name.

10. I break the power of seduction, deception, strong delusion, and lawlessness, in the name of Jesus.

11. I break and destroy the spirit of poverty, seduction, domestic violence and child abuse, in the mighty name of Jesus.

12. Father God, I loose Your perfect will and untapped power of the Holy Spirit over my life, my family, vision, prophetic words, possessions, finances, character, health, homes, and workplace, in the name of Jesus Christ. Amen.

# PRAYERS FOR OUTREACH MINISTRY

*Isaiah 52:7*
*How beautiful upon the mountains Are the feet of him who brings good news, Who proclaims peace, Who brings glad tidings of good things, Who proclaims salvation, Who says to Zion, "Your God reigns!"*

1. Father in Heaven, I pray for outreach ministers, missionaries and missionary workers around the world.
2. Bless these men and women who left the comfort of their homes and familiar surroundings to live in foreign lands and in unique environments for the sake of the gospel.
3. Prosper Your work in their hands. Open the hearts of the people they witness to, and draw multitudes to Jesus.
4. Confirm Your words in their mouths with signs and wonders following their preaching.
5. Grant them great favor before the government and the natives among whom they labor.
6. Provide for every one of their needs abundantly, emotionally, physically, financially, vocationally, and materially.
7. Keep them out of harm's way. Keep sickness and disease far away from them. Make them strong for

Yourself, O God, our Father.

8. I pray for Your grace and the anointing of Your Spirit to be multiplied upon their lives continually.

9. Touch the hearts of Your people and cause them to give generously to the work of missions and in support of these missionaries.

## SCRIPTURAL REFERENCES

| | |
|---|---|
| Matthew 28:19 | Go therefore and make disciples of all the nations, baptizing them in the name of the Father and of the Son and of the Holy Spirit, teaching them to observe all things that I have commanded you; and lo, I am with you always, even to the end of the age. Amen. |
| Mark 16:15 | And He said to them, Go into all the world and preach the gospel to every creature. |
| Jeremiah 1:7 | But the Lord said to me: "Do not say, 'I am a youth,' For you shall go to all to whom I send you, And whatever I command you, you shall speak. Do not be afraid of their faces, For I am with you to deliver you," says the Lord. |
| Jeremiah 1:9-10 | Then the Lord put forth His hand and |

| | touched my mouth, and the Lord said to me: "Behold, I have put My words in your mouth. See, I have this day set you over the nations and over the kingdoms, To root out and to pull down, To destroy and to throw down, To build and to plant." |
|---|---|
| Matthew 19:29 | And everyone who has left houses or brothers or sisters or father or mother or wife or children or lands, for My name's sake, shall receive a hundredfold, and inherit eternal life. |

# PRAYERS FOR UNITY

### Psalm 133:1
### Behold, how good and how pleasant it is For brethren to dwell together in unity!

1. Most High God, I approach Your throne right now, in the name of Jesus.
2. I come to plead for the spirit of unity to prevail among us, Your children, Your beloved, and among Your churches and leaders.
3. For united we stand, but divide we fall. Unite us together, O God, by the power of Your Spirit. Bind us together with a cord of love and unity that cannot be broken.
4. I command the wall of partition that has divided us for so long to fall down flat, after the order of the wall of Jericho.
5. Unite Your Church in love. Lord, arouse Your Church to a deep concern for the lost and perishing.
6. Give Your Church an intense burden and passion to rescue men and women, boys and girls from the flames of hell.
7. Stop, I pray, the meddling with sin that is common in the Church. Awaken Your Church to a higher standard of holiness and godliness. Without holiness, no eyes shall see You.

8. Help us to love one another sincerely and truly from our hearts. May we be our brother's keeper and seek the good of others. Amen.

# Forgiving Iniquity

*Lamentations 5:7*
*Our fathers sinned and are no more, but we bear their*
*iniquities.*

Father God, I come in the name of Jesus, and by the blood of the covenant, I enter into Your presence. I bring You worship and praise. There is none like unto You who keeps covenant with Your people. I bow at Your footstool and celebrate Your presence. You have declared in Your Word that our fathers have sinned, and they are no more, but we bear their reproaches that have fallen upon us. Our enemies have taken advantage of us because of the iniquities of our fathers, and they have afflicted us. You said in Your Word that You visit the iniquities of the fathers to the generations yet unborn.

Father, in the name of Jesus, I beseech You by Your Word. I appeal to Your covenant of mercy. You are the God of Heaven and Earth. You are the Great and Terrible God. Let Your ears be attentive to the prayer of the covenant. You are the God who keeps covenant and mercy with them who love You and keep Your Word. Father God, I humbly come before You; let Your ear be attentive to my prayer. Both my fathers and I have sinned. We have done foolishly and corrupted ourselves against You, and have not kept Your Word. For generations, servants have ruled over us because of this, and our inheritance has gone to strangers, our houses have gone to aliens. Some of our family members have become orphans, and fatherless, and some mothers have become widows. In the past, our fathers and mothers experienced the curse the enemy brought against them as a result of their iniquities. The servants have taken advantage of us, and there is none that shows us mercy. We have seen the same sicknesses that affected our fathers and mothers encroach upon us, and God forbid that we do not take a stand and ask You for mercy and forgiveness. If we don't turn to You, the enforcer of these curses will attack our sons and daughters. Father, You said in Your Word that You forgive the iniquities of the fathers to the third and fourth generations. Have mercy upon us, and forgive our fathers and mothers for our sake and our sons' and daughters' sake. O Lord, You live forever. Your throne is from generation to generation. Do not forget Your people, and do not forsake us forever.

Abba Father, Your Word says, "But there is forgiveness with thee, that thou mayest be feared." You alone forgive the iniquity of Your people and bless the work of their hands. You covered all of their sins. You have taken away Your wrath. You have turned Yourself from the fierceness of Your anger. Turn my captivity, O God of my salvation, and cause thine anger toward me to cease. Show me Your mercy, Father God. I turn unto You, according to Your Word, and I confess the sins and the iniquities of my fathers and mothers. Forgive, O God of my salvation; show me mercy and give me grace. Renew my days as of old. Do not reject me, Father. Do not be angry against us. Remember Your Word. You said if we transgress and turn to You, and keep Your words and do them, You will gather us from where we have been scattered, and You would forgive and heal our land. Father, we are Your people who You have redeemed by Your great power and by Your strong hand. You are my Redeemer and my Strong Tower; let Your ear be open and attentive to the prayers of Your servant, because I desire You and fear Your name. Forgive and prosper us.

O Precious Father, I pray You to hear Your servant this day and grant me mercy in Your eyes and in the sight of man. Let not my sons and daughters become outcasts, orphans, and vagabonds. Let not me or my children suffer the pain of these generational curses, because of the sins of our fathers. Come God; let's reason together. Let us not become a proverb and a byword. I exempt myself and my children from these curses, in the name of Jesus. Bless us and let not our sins be remembered by You. Holy Father, wash us clean with the blood of Jesus, and make us whole. Purify and satisfy us early with Your favor and mercy, and do us good all the days of our lives.

O Lord God, I have sinned, committed iniquity, acted wickedly, and have rebelled, even by deviating from Your commandments and from Your words. O Lord, confusion and shame rest on our faces because we have sinned against You. But to You, O Lord, my God is mercy and forgiveness, and Your love is everlasting. I beseech You loving Father, forgive and destroy the root of these iniquities in my bloodline by the blood of Jesus. Totally cleanse us by the blood of Your Son, Jesus, and set this family free from any curse that has come upon us as a result of this iniquity.

In the name of Jesus, I command all familiar spirits that are connected to these curses to be broken and destroyed. I command their assignments terminated. I command their activities in this family and in my life to cease, in the name of Jesus. Father, You said, You will not allow anyone to subvert my course in the land of the living. Let the enforcer of these curses be destroyed. Let deliverance come to this family. I command every curse over my life and family broken, and negative repetitive occurrences revoked, in the name of Jesus. I command every curse to end with me, and I put a stop to them by the blood of Jesus. In the name of Jesus, it will never be passed on to my children. They are free from all curses, in the name of Jesus. I love You, Jesus. You are my Lord, and You answer my prayer.

You said if I call, You will answer. Lord, be favorable to my family and me, and bless us indeed. Replace every curse with a blessing. Instead of sin, give us righteousness; instead of sickness, give us health; instead of poverty, give us wealth, and instead of death, give us life. Bring us out of captivity. You have always forgiven the iniquity of Your people when they asked You for forgiveness, and You have blessed them. Thank You for removing my iniquity. You have taken away

Your wrath. Thank You for forgiveness and for turning away from the fierceness of Your anger. You have shown me mercy. You have granted me Your salvation. You have granted me life and favor. The visitation of Your Holy Spirit has preserved my spirit.

# Come Appealing to the Blood

Because of the shed blood of Jesus, the blood of the covenant and the blood that speaks better than that of Abel, I declare right now that based on the Word of God, the iniquities that gave the devil the legal right into and over my family have been forgiven. Therefore, the devil and his demoniacs have no legal rights to hold my family anymore. Devil, in the name of Jesus, you cannot harm my family or me anymore. Satan, the blood of Jesus is against you.

The blood of the everlasting covenant speaks for me. The blood of the Lamb speaks peace; where there was confusion, You have given harmony; where there were curses, You have given blessings; where there was danger, You have given protection; where there was death, You have given life, and You have given promotion where there were demotion, stagnancy, and setbacks. Let the blood continue to speak for me. The blood of Jesus is my answer. The blood of the everlasting covenant is my refuge and my fortress. I overcome the devil and his agents by the blood of Jesus and by the word of my testimony, and I ask that the Holy Spirit will enforce the work of the blood in my life. I declare victory over every satanic power by the blood of Jesus.

I am free from the devil's power and control. Thank God Almighty, I am free, in Jesus' name. I enforce the blessing of El-Shaddai by the anointing of the Holy Spirit, in the name of

Jesus, over my family right now. I declare by the mandate of the Word of God that we shall never be the same. I loosen the supernatural power of God into motion in my life and family, counteracting every satanic stronghold and every demonic agenda. I loosen the glory of Almighty God over my life. I declare that I will never lack because the Lord God is my shield and exceeding great reward, in Jesus' name. Amen.

# LET GOD ARISE

I have put the following scriptures together for you, so that in every situation and in all opposition and warfare, you can use these scriptural verses to invoke the presence and the power of God. Meditate on them, and allow the Holy Spirit to reveal the depth of these revelational truths in warfare prayers to your spirit.

1.  Let God arise, let His enemies be scattered: let them also that hate Him flee before Him. As smoke is driven away, so drive them away: as wax melteth before the fire, so let the wicked perish at the presence of God. But let the righteous be glad; let them rejoice before God: yea, let them exceedingly rejoice (Psalm 68: 1-3).
2.  They have now compassed us in our steps: they have set their eyes bowing down to the Earth; like as a lion that is greedy of his prey, and as it were a young lion lurking in secret places. Arise, O Lord, disappoint him, cast him down: deliver my soul from the wicked, which is thy sword (Psalm 17: 11-13).
3.  For the oppression of the poor, for the sighing of the needy, now will I arise, saith the Lord; I will set him in safety from him that puffeth at him (Psalm 12:5).
4.  Arise for our help, and redeem us for thy mercies' sake (Psalm 44:26).
5.  Arise, O God, plead thine own cause: remember how

the foolish man reproacheth thee daily (Psalm 74:22).

6. Thou shalt arise, and have mercy upon Zion: for the time to favor her, yea, the set time, is come (Psalms 102:13).

7. Arise for our help, and redeem us for thy mercies' sake (Psalm 44:26).

8. Arise, O Lord; O God, lift up thine hand: forget not the humble (Psalm 10:12).

9. Arise, O Lord; let not man prevail: let the heathen be judged in thy sight. Put them in fear, O Lord: that the nations may know themselves to be but men. Selah (Psalm 9:19-20).

10. Arise, O Lord, in thine anger, lift up thyself because of the rage of mine enemies: and awake for me to the judgment that thou hast commanded. So shall the congregation of the people compass thee about: for their sakes therefore return thou on high (Psalm 7:6-7).

11. Arise, O Lord; save me, O my God: for thou hast smitten all mine enemies upon the cheek bone; thou hast broken the teeth of the ungodly. Salvation belongeth unto the Lord: thy blessing is upon thy people. Selah (Psalm 3:7-8).

12. Arise, O God, judge the Earth: for thou shalt inherit all nations (Psalm 82:8).

13. We will go into his tabernacles: we will worship at his footstool. Arise, O Lord, into thy rest; thou, and the ark of thy strength. Let thy priests be clothed with

righteousness; and let thy saints shout for joy (Psalm 132:7-9).

14. For the Lord hath chosen Zion; he hath desired it for his habitation. This is my rest for ever: here will I dwell; for I have desired it. I will abundantly bless her provision: I will satisfy her poor with bread. I will also clothe her priests with salvation: and her saints shall shout aloud for joy. There will I make the horn of David to bud: I have ordained a lamp for mine anointed. His enemies will I clothe with shame: but upon himself shall his crown. flourish (Psalm 13:2-18).

# I'm Walking Under Open Heavens and Going Through Open Doors

1. Father in Heaven, I thank You for the mercies and blessings of this life. I give You all the glory and express my appreciation to You.
2. Give me the grace to walk under open Heavens and go through all the open doors You have set before me.
3. Grant me the grace of deliberate, ordinate progress to experience miracles and a purposeful divine release.
4. Let there be a divine decree and guaranteed enforcement of favor for progress in all areas of my life.
5. Let the Heavens over me be opened, and let me see visions of God. Let the Heavens open over me; let me see the Spirit of God descend like a dove and settle upon me permanently.
6. Let the Heavens open over me, and let me see Jesus standing at the right hand of God. Let this vision encourage and embolden me to do as occasion serves me, and fulfill my destiny, in Jesus' name.
7. Windows of Heaven, be opened and pour blessings in my life more than I have room enough to receive. Let me experience the abundance of God.
8. Lord, rend the Heavens and come down that the

mountains and challenges of my life will melt.

9. Heavens, hear the Word of God, and open, in Jesus' name. Open over my life, flash a divine bright light on me and cause me to see clearly. Let your light be permanent and be the street light of my life that will deliver me from the darkness.

10. Heavens, drop down dew and refresh my life. Water the garden of my life, and let me bring forth fruit.

11. Angels of the living God, open every prison door I have been locked behind and bring me out.

12. Let a great spiritual earthquake happen, and let the foundations of my prison be shaken, and all doors be opened for me to walk through.

13. Great door, open to me, and let God overcome the adversaries of my open doors so I can walk through.

14. Great door, open to me, and let God overcome the adversaries of my open doors so I can walk through them to a better life, in Jesus' name.

15. Lord Jesus, open doors in my life that no man can shut forevermore, and give me the grace to walk through them.

16. Let the door of Heaven be opened to me so that I can begin to hear Your divine conversations in a new way.

17. Let me experience permanent open Heavens.

18. Let all the doors of my blessings be opened in every area of my life.

19. I decree that open Heavens and open doors be activated in my life, in Jesus' mighty name. Amen.

# PRAYERS OF CONSECRATION

## Psalm 51:10
*Create in me a clean heart, O God, And renew a steadfast spirit within me.*

1. Almighty God, I come to consecrate my life to You as a living sacrifice. Lord, I lay my life on Your altar. Take me, break me, mold me and use me.
2. Lord, create in me a clean heart, O God, and renew a right spirit within me.
3. Consecrate me now to Your service, O Lord, by the power of grace divine. Let my soul look up with a steadfast hope, and my will be lost in Yours.
4. I wholly surrender my life to You, to Your service, to Your purpose and to Your calling.
5. Lord, as the deer thirsts and runs after the water, so my soul longs for You.
6. Lord, keep me from sin. Teach me how to walk wisely. Enable me to guard my mind against errors, my heart against wrong feelings, and my life against evil actions.
7. Father, help me to live for You. I want to be like Jesus. Let the same mind that was in Christ be in me, O God, my Father.
8. Let others see Jesus in me. Help me to reflect the light I received from Christ. Lord, make me holy. Give me a

humble heart and a gentle spirit.

9. Let me never bring shame nor reproach to Your name. Help me to be a good ambassador for Jesus and a faithful servant of Yours.

10. Keep me from falling, and present me faultless before Your presence. O Lord, work in me to will and to do Your own good pleasure.

11. Lord, sanctify me. Make me an obedient servant of Yours. Write Your law upon my heart and upon my mind.

# Prayers of Thanksgiving

*Psalm 95:2*
*Let us come before His presence with thanksgiving; let us shout joyfully to Him with psalms.*

1. Great and awesome God, I want to thank You sincerely from my heart for saving my soul and snatching me from the jaws of death and destruction.
2. I thank You for sending Jesus Christ, Your Son, to die on the cross of Calvary for my sins.
3. I thank You for my salvation. I thank You for Your grace, Your tender mercies and Your loving kindness.
4. I thank You for the gift of Your Spirit. I thank You for Your anointing upon my life.
5. I thank You for Your Word, the Bible, and the great promise contained therein.
6. I thank You for Your great deliverance, provision, protection and divine providence.
7. I thank You for what You have done for me in the past. I thank You for what You are doing in my life right now. I thank You for all that You will do for me in the future.
8. I thank You for my job, ministry, my children, my spouse, family members, both near and far, my parents, and my business.
9. If I have a thousand tongues, they are not enough to

thank You for all Your goodness in my life.

10. Savior Divine, accept my humble thanks that comes from a heart that loves You. You are very dear to my heart, O Jesus, the lover of my soul.

11. I will adore and magnify Your holy name. As long as You lend me breath, Your praise shall continually be in my mouth. In Jesus' mighty name. Amen.

## SCRIPTURAL REFERENCES

| | |
|---|---|
| Psalm 100:4 | Enter into His gates with thanksgiving, And into His courts with praise. Be thankful to Him, and bless His name. |

# Prayers of Divine Healing and Health

## Isaiah 53:5

*But He was wounded for our transgressions, He was bruised for our iniquities; the chastisement of our peace was upon Him; and with his stripes we are healed.*

1. Father in the name of Jesus, I bless Your name that I can say from the bottom of my heart "Abba Father."
2. It is my greatest joy that I have become Your child by faith in Christ Jesus.
3. Great Physician, I bring You my iniquities, and by Your stripes, I am healed. I receive my healing by faith right now, in Jesus' name.
4. Now Father, I take my authority and I claim back this temple, in the name of Jesus. I command every evil, foul and unclean spirit to leave this place, in Jesus' name. I bind every strongman, principality, demonic power, ruler of darkness, and the spiritual hosts of wickedness in Heavenly places over this temple.
5. I renounce, break, and loose this temple from any and every dark spirit, evil influence, satanic bondage, evil curse, charm, vex, hex, spell, jinx, bewitchment, charismatic witchcraft prayer, witchcraft, sorcery, psychic heredity, demonic hold, psychic power, bondage and all self-imposed, generational, or

temporary curses that have been put on this temple from any person or persons or from any occult source, or from any sin, transgression, iniquity, occult or psychic involvement committed by this temple. The curse causeless shall not come.

6. I rebuke symptoms, abnormalities, irregularities in any part of my body. I render your power over me impotent, in Jesus' name.

7. I rebuke the demonic objects behind any outbreaks, epidemic and pandemic. I bind the stubborn spirits of diseases, the cold-hearted diseases, the gloominess of diseases, the bodied-hostage of disease, the demonic blood pollution and organ failure of diseases, in the name of Jesus.

8. I bind every sickness and disease that runs through my bloodline.

9. I destroy the yokes of high blood pressure, heart disease, all blood diseases, and all forms of cancer, in the name of Jesus.

10. In the name of Jesus, I bind breast cancers, emphysemas, lung cancers, bone cancers and any other form of cancer from the pit of hell.

11. I bind the demonic entities behind these infirmities.

12. You are Jehovah Ropheka. Father, You are my healer.

13. I loose the anointing against leukemia and cancers that attack the skin and liver, in the name of Jesus.

14. I claim my liberty, healing, and health.

15. I bind the spirit of pneumonia and asthma from my family, in the name of Jesus.

16. I bind all forms of paralysis and kidney failure.
17. I dominate sickness and disease, and take authority over every demonic destruction of the physical man.
18. I declare that there is a shift in the atmosphere; where there is death, there will be the wind of life, in Jesus' name.
19. I know that my problem and crisis situation are a divine announcement.
20. I call down the thunder and fire of God to burn to ashes every burden of the enemy that has put a blockage in my spiritual, physical and/or financial health.
21. I come against every spirit of infirmity. I bind and cast you out of my body, in Jesus' name.
22. I command all harmful bacteria that is infecting any part of my body to wither and die, in the name of Jesus.
23. I release the anointing of the Holy Spirit to go through my central nervous system, bones, marrow, veins, bloodstream, heart, lungs and kidneys. Purge and flush out any harmful organism that doesn't belong in my body.
24. Your Word is Your medicine. O God, You are in the business of supernatural healing.
25. I touch the hem of Your garment and receive healing. There is no restriction to how You can do work in my life.
26. This threatening disease is no match for the blood of Jesus.

27. I lay hands on myself and command the healing power of God to flow from the top of my head to the soles of my feet, and make me whole— spirit, soul and body. I am the healed and not the sick. Amen.

28. Master, touch, heal, and make me whole, in the name of Jesus.

29. Heal every complicated health hazard in my body.

30. I apply the blood of Jesus over my life, and command the effects of years of physical, emotional, verbal and mental abuse to be healed, in Jesus' name.

31. Thank You for the grace to be healthy enough to manifest Your desire that I become a sign and a wonder.

32. Thank You, Lord Jesus, for healing me this day. I give You praise, I give You glory, I give You honor and thanks forever. Amen.

# HEALING REINFORCEMENT PRAYERS

Father God, in the name of Jesus, the name that is above all names, who will answer me and show me great and mighty things. I ask for a complete restoration and healing of my body, according to Your Word, promises, covenant, and will. Lord Jesus, You paid the price for me on the cross, along with the fullness of salvation's redemption with all the benefits of healing and abundant life.

In the name of Jesus, I am redeemed from sickness. For sickness, He has given me health. I am the healed and not the sick. I am satisfied with long life, according to His Word, and He shall show me His salvation, deliverance, and blessings. I will walk in divine health, and I am alive to righteousness, but dead to sin. I hope and trust in God, for I shall praise Him who is the health of my countenance. I am in Christ; I am a new creature. Old things are passed away; behold, all things have become new. God forgives all my iniquities. He heals all my diseases. He redeems my life from destruction. He crowns me with loving kindness and tender mercies. God keeps His Word to me. He watches over His Word to perform it. Manifest Your greatness in all areas of my life.

I now repent for any open door that allowed the enemy of deception, sickness, and infirmity to enter my life. I cast every one of these spirits to the pit, in the mighty name of Jesus. I decree that no weapon formed against me shall prosper, and that by the stripes of Jesus, I am healed and freed from all disease, infirmities, self-imposed curses, and labels placed upon my life. I believe in the resurrection power of Christ Jesus, the Creator of my spirit, soul and body, and I command that power to be restored to me completely as the temple of the living God. I have a call, purpose and destiny to fulfill, ordained by the living God to heal the sick and cast out demons. I am a sign and a wonder; I am touched, healed and changed by the Everlasting Father of love. I decree every blood vessel, organ, tissue and bone be cleansed and healed by the blood of Christ Jesus. I thank You, Father, for Your mercy, grace and covenant in answering my requests. All Glory belongs to You!

## SCRIPTURAL REFERENCES

### Healing

| | |
|---|---|
| 1 Peter 2:24 | Who Himself bore our sins in His own body on the tree, that we, having died to sins, might live for righteousness—by whose [a]stripes you were healed. |
| Psalm 30:2 | O Lord my God, I cried out to You, and You healed me. |
| Psalm 34:19 | Many are the afflictions of the righteous, but the Lord delivers him out of them all. |
| Psalm 103:3 | Who forgives all your iniquities, who heals |

| | all your diseases. |
|---|---|
| 3 John 1:2 | Beloved, I pray that you may prosper in all things and be in health, just as your soul prospers. |
| Matthew 8:16-17 | When evening had come, they brought to Him many who were demon-possessed. And He cast out the spirits with a word, and healed all who were sick, that it might be fulfilled which was spoken by Isaiah the prophet, saying: "He Himself took our infirmities And bore our sicknesses." |
| Romans 8:11 | But if the Spirit of Him who raised Jesus from the dead dwells in you, He who raised Christ from the dead will also give life to your mortal bodies [a]through His Spirit who dwells in you. |
| Jeremiah 17:14 | Heal me, O Lord, and I shall be healed; Save me, and I shall be saved, For You are my praise. |
| Exodus 23:25 | So You shall serve the Lord Your God, and He will bless Your bread and Your water. And I will take sickness away from the midst of You. |

### Broken Heart / Pain

| Psalm 25:18 | Look on my affliction and my pain, And forgive all my sins. |
|---|---|

| Psalm 147:3 | He heals the brokenhearted And binds up their wounds. |
| Isaiah 53:4 | Surely He has borne our griefs And carried our sorrows. |
| John 14:27 | Peace I leave with you, My peace I give to you; not as the world gives do I give to you. Let not your heart be troubled, neither let it be afraid. |

## Bone Disease

| Psalm 6:2 | Have mercy on me, O Lord, for I am weak; O Lord, heal me, for my bones are troubled. |
| Psalm 34:20 | He guards all his bones; Not one of them is broken. |
| Isaiah 58:11 | The Lord will guide you continually, And satisfy your soul in drought, And strengthen your bones; You shall be like a watered garden, And like a spring of water, whose waters do not fail. |

## Pregnancy

| Exodus 23:26 | No one shall suffer miscarriage or be barren in your land; I will fulfill the number of your days. |

## Child Birth

| | |
|---|---|
| Isaiah 66:7 | Before she was in labor, she gave birth; Before her pain came, She delivered a male child. |
| 1 Timothy 2:15 | Nevertheless she will be saved in childbearing if they continue in faith, love, and holiness, with self-control. |

## Fever

| | |
|---|---|
| Luke 4:38 – 39 | Now He arose from the synagogue and entered Simon's house. But Simon's wife's mother was [a]sick with a high fever, and they made request of Him concerning her. So He stood over her and rebuked the fever, and it left her. And immediately she arose and served them. |

## Heart Disease

| | |
|---|---|
| Psalm 27:14 | Wait on the Lord; Be of good courage, And He shall strengthen your heart; Wait, I say, on the Lord! |
| Psalm 31:24 | Be of good courage, And He shall strengthen your heart, All you who hope in the Lord. |
| Psalm 73:26 | My flesh and my heart fail; But God is the strength of my heart and my portion forever. |

## Sleeplessness

| | |
|---|---|
| Psalm 4:8 | I will both lie down in peace, and sleep; For You alone, O Lord, make me dwell in safety. |
| Proverbs 3:24 | When you lie down, you will not be afraid; Yes, you will lie down and your sleep will be sweet. |
| Ecclesiastes 5:12 | The sleep of a laboring man is sweet, Whether he eats little or much; But the abundance of the rich will not permit him to sleep. |
| Psalm 34:7 | The angel of the Lord encamps all around those who fear Him, And delivers them. |

## Strokes/Muscular Dystrophy/Palsy/Multiple Sclerosis

| | |
|---|---|
| Psalm 116:8 | For You have delivered my soul from death, My eyes from tears, And my feet from falling. |
| 1 Samuel 2:4 | The bows of the mighty men are broken, And those who stumbled are girded with strength. |
| Psalm 56:13 | For You have delivered my soul from death. Have You not kept my feet from falling, That I may walk before God In the light of the living? |
| Psalm 145:14 | The Lord upholds all who fall, And raises up all who are bowed down. |

## Poisoning

| Mark 16:18 | They will take up serpents; and if they drink anything deadly, it will by no means hurt them; they will lay hands on the sick, and they will recover. |
|---|---|

## Diabolical Poisoning

| Isaiah 54:17 | No weapon formed against you shall prosper, And every tongue which rises against you in judgment You shall condemn. |
|---|---|

## Stammering/Stuttering

| Isaiah 32:4 | Also the heart of the rash will understand knowledge, and the tongue of the stammers will be ready to speak plainly. |
|---|---|
| Mark 7:32-35 | Then they brought to Him one who was deaf and had an impediment in his speech, and they begged Him to put His hand on him. And He took him aside from the multitude, and put His fingers in his ears, and He spat and touched his tongue. Then, looking up to Heaven, He sighed, and said to him, "Ephphatha," that is, "Be opened." Immediately his ears were opened, and the [a]impediment of his tongue was loosed, and he spoke plainly. |

## Chronic Fatigue/Tiredness and Weakness

| Isaiah 40:29 | He gives power to the weak, and to those who have no might He increases strength. |
|---|---|
| Isaiah 40:31 | But those who wait on the Lord shall renew their strength; They shall mount up with wings like eagles, They shall run and not be weary, They shall walk and not faint. |

## Stomach Ulcers

| Jeremiah 30:17 | For I will restore health to you And heal you of Your wounds,' says the Lord. |
|---|---|

## Tumors/Growth

| Matthew 15:13 | But He answered and said, "Every plant which My heavenly Father has not planted will be uprooted." |
|---|---|

# PRAYERS OF RESTORATION

*Job 42:10*
*And the Lord restored Job's losses when he prayed for his friends. Indeed the Lord gave Job twice as much as he had before.*

1. Dear Heavenly Father, I thank You for You are the God of restoration. You restored Job's losses and gave him twice what he had before.
2. Restore my spirit, my soul, and my body to perfect wholeness from the years of abuse.
3. Touch my mind, my emotions and my conscience, and restore my sensitivity and tenderness.
4. Restore my family, my career, my finances, my business, my children and all lost opportunities.
5. Restore great favor where favor is needed, and give me favor with men and with You.
6. God is the Master Builder and He is the Restorer.
7. God, please restore me and bring me back from underneath the enemy's dirt and grime.
8. I pronounce restitution over my life, according to Proverbs 6:31. All that was taken, will be returned seven-fold. My enemy is headed toward bankruptcy.
9. If the enemy has tried to put depression and heaviness on me, I'm getting ready for seven-fold "joy."

10. If the enemy has tried to put sickness on me, I'm getting ready for seven-fold "health."

11. If the enemy has tried to put debt and lack on me, I'm getting ready for seven-fold "prosperity and provision."

12. If the enemy has tried to put fear and anxiety on me, I'm getting ready for seven-fold "faith."

13. If the enemy has tried to put bondage and addiction on me, I'm getting ready for seven-fold "freedom."

14. This means that Satan is defeated on his own terms.

15. God is opening doors and opening Heaven, which no man can shut. He is faithful. If He said it, He will do it.

16. Remove the guilt, the reproach, the shame and the pain of my past misdeeds permanently from me.

17. Great Physician, I bring You my wounds and bruises, my sicknesses and diseases. Touch, heal and make me whole, from the top of my head to the soles of my feet.

18. Restore and rekindle the first love I had for You, Lord. Restore my passion for You, and restore my compassion for Your people.

19. Restore my calling, my ministry, my vision and my talents. Do not let my vision die, nor my love for You grow cold, in Jesus' name. Amen!

# PRAYERS OF PROTECTION

*Psalm 34:7*
*The angel of the Lord encamps all around those who fear*
*Him, And delivers them.*

1. Heavenly Father, You are my Hiding Place, Shelter, Refuge, and Deliverer.
2. Protect me, O Lord, from the violent ones who have purposed in their hearts to hurt my soul. Deliver me from my enemy, O God, and defend me against them that rise up against me.
3. Let not the foot of pride come against me, nor the hand of the wicked remove me, O Lord God, for I put my trust in You.
4. Draw out Your sword, stand in the way, and stop them who are in hot pursuit of my soul to destroy it. Raise a hedge of protection around me—a hedge that no enemy or evil can penetrate.
5. Oh Lord, take hold of shield and buckler, stand up, and help me. For as the mountain encompasses Jerusalem, so the Lord encompasses those who love Him.
6. Send Your angels to be my bodyguards to protect me against the attack and the assault of the wicked ones.
7. Cause me to escape the snares, traps, and nets my enemies have secretly hidden for my soul.

8. Bring my soul out of trouble caused by those who hate me, for I put my trust in You. Make my enemy turn back and run away from me. For it is written, "They shall come against me one way, and flee seven ways."

9. Lord, I have heard the slander of many, and fear is on every side. Deliver me from all my fears. Make Your face to shine upon me and save me for Your mercy's sake. Let me not be ashamed.

10. Set me at safety from the braggarts. For it is written, he that digs a pit shall fall into it. Let the wicked fall into their own pits that they have dug, and let them be taken by the nets they have set. Amen.

Thank You, Father, for the answers to my prayers. For all these and much more, I ask in the name of Your Son, Jesus Christ. Amen.

# PROTECTION CONFESSIONS

I overcome the devil by the blood of the Lamb and by the word of my testimony. The blood of Jesus covers and protects me from the enemy. I am totally secured, in Jesus' name. The angels of the Lord encamp around my dwelling, just as the mountains surround Jerusalem. I am engraved in the palm of the Lord. No man can snatch me out of God's hand. I am the apple of His eye.

My life is hidden in Christ and God. I am totally protected. The everlasting God is my refuge, and underneath me are His everlasting arms. He commands His angels to take charge over me in all my ways, lest I dash my foot against a stone.

The enemy shall be as the grass upon the house-tops, which withers before it grows up. The Lord rises up to my defense all the time, and He keeps me. God is my protection. He that keeps me never sleeps, and He never slumbers. The Lord is a shadow on my right side. The sun shall not smite me by day nor the moon by night. The Lord orders my steps, and He delights in my way. He preserves my going forth and coming in all the days of my life. I am protected from diseases and sickness that waste at noonday. I lay down and sleep. I awake, for the Lord sustains me, and His right hand shall save me.

I will not be afraid of thousands of people that set themselves against me round about. The blood of Jesus speaks life and security for me. I shall not die but live. The Lord goes before me and makes the crooked places straight. He breaks into pieces the gates of brass and cuts asunder the bars of iron. The Lord gives me the treasures of darkness and hidden riches of secret places. I lift up my face without spot; I am steadfast, and I am not fearful. The enemy cannot break down my wall, for my defenses are solid. I am hidden from the scourge of the tongue. I am not afraid of destruction when it comes, for the Lord is my defense. He secures my feet from being taken.

At destruction and famine, I will laugh. I will not be afraid of demonic entities. The blood of Jesus protects me. The blood of Jesus speaks for me. The blood speaks protection and safety for me. I am abounding in blessings. When I pass through the waters, God will be with me. When I walk through the fire, I shall not be burned, neither shall the flame kindle upon me. For the Lord, my God, the Holy One of Israel, my Savior, is with me.

I am precious in the Lord's sight. I have been honorable, and the Lord loves me. Therefore, He gives men for me and people for my life. I cannot be cursed because I am blessed of God. Surely there is no enchantment against me, neither is there any divination against me. Behold, God had grafted me upon the palms of His hands. The Lord delivers me out of all affliction. He keeps all my bones, and not one of them is broken. Evil shall slay the wicked, and they that hate me shall be desolate. The Lord redeems the soul of His servants, and none of them that trust in Him shall be desolate. By my God, I run through a troop and I leap over walls. I leap over walls of limitations, restrictions, oppositions, and lack. The Lord contends with him that contends with me.

## SCRIPTURAL REFERENCES

| | |
|---|---|
| Psalms 91:1 | He who dwells in the secret place of the Most High Shall abide under the shadow of the Almighty. |
| Psalms 46:1-2 | God is our refuge and strength, A very present help in trouble. Therefore we will not fear, Even though the Earth be removed, And though the mountains be carried into the midst of the sea. |
| Psalms 91:9-11 | Because you have made the Lord, who is my refuge, Even the Most High, your dwelling place, No evil shall befall you, Nor shall any plague come near your dwelling; For He shall give His angels charge over you, To keep you in all your ways. |
| Psalm 97:10 | You who love the Lord, hate evil; He preserves the souls of His saints; He delivers them out of the hand of the wicked. |
| Psalms 121:7-8 | The Lord shall [a]preserve you from all evil; He shall preserve your soul. The Lord shall preserve your going out and your coming in |

| | |
|---|---|
| | from this time forth, and even forevermore. |
| Isaiah 32:18 | My people will dwell in a peaceful habitation, In secure dwellings, and in quiet resting places. |
| Isaiah 59:19 | When the enemy comes in like a flood, the Spirit of the Lord will lift up a standard against him. |

# PRAYERS AGAINST REJECTION

In the name of Jesus, I take my dominion and authority, and I forgive every person and everything that has happened in my life that has opened the door to rejection and every spirit associated with it. I apply the blood of Jesus in these places, and I command that spirit of rejection, and every spirit associated with it, along with every emotional soul tie spirit, old fragments, and broken pieces to loose and leave me, and go to the pit, in the name of Jesus.

I sever the emotional attachment with every person, place, thing, smell, taste, trauma, the writing on the walls, and event in my life associated with the spirit of rejection, and I command them to loose and leave me now, and go to the pit because the anointing of Christ has destroyed every yoke. I am washed by the blood of the Lamb. I have a purpose, a destiny and a calling. I have a charge to keep and a God to glorify. I am more than a conqueror; none of these things shall move me, and He who is in me is greater than he who is in the world because I carry and accept the love of God for myself and for others. He is my Abba Father, in Jesus' name. Amen.

# TERRITORIAL PRAYER

In the mighty name of Jesus, I take my authority. I bind every foul, unclean, seducing, and hindering spirit of darkness. I bind every strongman, principality, and territorial spirit of the waters, land, air, and sea. I bind every spirit of witchcraft, sorcery, occult, divination, anti-Christ, false religion, bondage, and addiction. I bind every spirit of Jezebel, Ahab, Baal, and queen of Heaven. I bind all mind-binding spirits, mind-controlling spirits, familiar spirits, and spirits of rebellion, gossip, criticism, offense, division, and strife. I bind all spirits of immaturity, cobra, leviathan, spirits of fear, anxiety, stress, worry, death, murder, theft, and lying. I bind every spirit of deception, anger, hatred, jealousy, pride, arrogance, and corruption. I bind all spirits of perversion, whoredom, adultery, molestation, incest, abuse, pedophilia, identity crisis, and the spirits of greed. I bind every spirit of covetousness, love of money, false worship, soulish prayers, idolatry, debt, lack, poverty, and the prince of the power of air. I bind all spirits of insanity, depression, oppression, self-destruction, unforgiveness, laziness, compromise, coarse jesting, foul mouth, unbelief, doubt, and complacency. I bind all spirits of resentment, revenge, judgment, exaggeration, delusion, blindness, apathy, apostasy, and the Judas spirit of betrayal. I bind the spirits of multiple personalities, miscarriage, self-sabotage, misconception, blindness, and deaf and dumb spirits. I bind every inherited spirit, spirit of infirmity, and any other spirit under the authority of Satan's kingdom.

I bind, blind, mute, and deafen these spirits, in the name of Jesus, cutting off their communication and driving them out the territories of myself, my spouse, children, family members, and co-workers. I drive demonic spirits out of our neighborhoods, schools, places of employment, and local/city/state offices. I command these spirits to loosen our families, relationships, possessions, homes, health, seeds, harvest, inheritances, finances, jobs, and projects. I loose our destiny, dreams, vision, calling, ministries, outreaches, whatever we put our hands to, and wherever we set our feet to go today. I also bind all territorial spirits that come against my relationship with the Lord, the move of the Holy Spirit, and the angels working on my behalf. I do all this in the authority and name of Jesus Christ. I cast all these spirits into the pit and command them not to return. I apply the blood of Jesus to all these territories and ask for the assistance of the angels in protecting them. In Jesus' name. Amen.

# PRAYERS OF PROSPERITY AND MATERIAL BLESSINGS

### 3 John 2
*Beloved, I pray that you may prosper in all things and be in health, just as your soul prospers.*

1. Almighty God, I come before You, in the name of Jesus. I thank You for Your goodness, tender mercies, provision, and providence.
2. Lord, enlarge my coast, gird me with strength, and grant me great favor before all men.
3. Riches and honor come from You; silver and gold are Yours, and You own the cattle on a thousand hills. Bring me into a wealthy place for Your name and glory's sake.
4. Financial prosperity is flowing my way and continually growing.
5. I declare seven income streams for millionaires and billionaires is my portion: (Earned Income, Profit Income, Interest Income, Dividend Income, Capital Gains, and Royalty Income).
6. My economic territory is rapidly expanding and ever-increasing.
7. I shall believe His prophets and prosper.
8. I shall receive Your power to get wealth.
9. I shall sow seeds and believe You for a mighty return.

10. I am like a tree planted by streams of water, always producing fruit, and my leaves never fall.

11. Everything I do will be successful. Whatever I start will finish with success.

12. I take authority over unnecessary taxes, and I release integrity to our elected officials. Your will be done!

13. The work of my hands is blessed. I will prosper in my job, career, ministry, business, and marketplace.

14. You delight in the prosperity of Your servants, among whom I am. You will not withhold any good thing from me.

15. I ask You, in the name of Jesus, to prosper my soul, spirit, body, finances, family, children, job, and everything that pertains to me.

16. I come against the devourer, the cankerworms, the caterpillars, and the locusts. I paralyze their work in my finances. The Lord rebukes you, you wicked spirits, that cause lack—be gone, in Jesus' name.

17. I ask that doors of financial opportunities be opened to me. I walk through those doors right now by faith, in Jesus' name.

18. Let there be showers of blessings. Lord, You are my Shepherd, and I shall not want. Lord, cause everything that I am involved in to prosper.

19. I am the head and not the tail. I am at the top and never at the bottom.

20. There's no task, assignment, or project too large or too overwhelming for me.

21. I am under an open Heaven, and Your blessings are poured upon my life, in Jesus' name.
22. Open doors are my portion. I have favor wherever I go and with whomever I meet.
23. I have favor with a suitable workplace. I have pleasant colleagues and a friendly boss. My salary and benefits are satisfying.
24. This is my season of divine mergers.
25. This is my season to be an entrepreneur ("Receive the mantle of Lidia").
26. This is my season to become a multi-millionaire.
27. This is my season to be anointed in the marketplace.
28. This is my season of abundance.
29. This is my season of advancement.
30. This is my season of divine appointments.
31. This is my season to possess my possessions.
32. This is my season to give the Lord an external and an unconditional yes.
33. This is my season of overflow.
34. Make me strong and prosperous for Your name's sake. Turn to me, O Lord, my Great Provider, and show me a token of Your love.
35. Let Your right hand hold me up and Your gentleness make me great. Enlarge my feet under me, O Lord. In Jesus' name. Amen.

## SCRIPTURAL REFERENCES

| Job 36:11 | If they obey and serve Him, They shall spend their days in prosperity, And their |
|---|---|

| | years in pleasures. |
|---|---|
| Joshua 1:8 | This Book of the Law shall not depart from your mouth, but you shall meditate in it day and night, that you may observe to do according to all that is written in it. For then you will make your way prosperous, and then you will have good success. |
| Psalm 35:27 | Let the Lord be magnified, Who has pleasure in the prosperity of His servant. |
| Psalm 84:11 | For the Lord God is a sun and shield; The Lord will give grace and glory; No good thing will He withhold From those who walk uprightly. |
| Isaiah 45:3 | I will give you the treasures of darkness And hidden riches of secret places, That you may know that I, the Lord, Who call you by your name, Am the God of Israel. |
| Proverbs 8:21 | That I may cause those who love me to inherit wealth, That I may fill their treasuries. |
| Psalm 92:12 | The righteous shall flourish like a palm tree, He shall grow like a cedar in Lebanon. |
| Deuteronomy 8:18 | And you shall remember the Lord, your God, for it is He who gives you power to get wealth. |

# PRAYER ABOUT MONEY

*Ecclesiastes 10:19*
*A feast is made for laughter, And wine makes merry; But money answers everything.*

1. Great and Mighty God, the Creator and Owner of Heaven and Earth, to You be glory, honor, power, and all majesty.
2. Father, all that I am and have, I have received from You.
3. Lord, provide for my needs so that I will be able to do what You have called me to do. Help me to be a blessing to others in need.
4. Lord, do not delay Your blessings and promises that You have caused me to build my hope upon.
5. In the multitude of my needs, let my silence speak to You. Lord, hurry to help me. Rescue me, for I don't know what to do or who to turn to but You.
6. I have a paid-in-full anointing, and I am debt free, in Jesus' name.
7. Thank You Lord, for my God shall supply all my needs according to His riches in glory by Christ Jesus. Amen.

## Material Blessings Confession

Christ has redeemed me from the curse of the law; I am redeemed from the curse of poverty. For poverty, He has given me riches. I am blessed financially. God lives through me.

For ashes, God has given me beauty; for mourning, He has given me the oil of joy; for the spirit of heaviness, He has given me the garment of praise. I am the planting of the Lord. Because I obey and serve Him, I shall spend my days in prosperity, and my years in pleasures. The blessings of the Lord upon my life have made me rich. The Lord delights in my prosperity, and Abraham's blessings are mine.

Money comes to me now. I am favored by the Lord to receive from men now. My God delights in my prosperity. I am not poor, but I am rich. I am out of debt now! My needs are met, not according to my salary, but according to His riches in glory. Money comes to me from everywhere. The Lord is my Shepherd; I shall not want. I shall not want for money, I shall not want for power, and I shall not want for favor. I have plenty more to put in store. I am blessed and I am a blessing. I am prosperous. I am rich. I am wealthy, in the name of Jesus. My money is on its way. It is on its way now. God has promoted me now. I have increased now. I am extremely successful now. I am loaded with ideas and money. I am empowered by God to get wealth, and I have it now. I will never lack. I bind the spirit of setbacks from my life. I possess my possessions now.

I am like a tree planted by the rivers of water. I bring forth my fruit in due season; my leaf does not wither, and whatsoever I do prospers. I shout for joy. I am glad, and I favor God's righteous cause. I will say continually that the Lord is magnified who has pleasure in my prosperity. The rod of the wicked rest not upon my lot; I, therefore, do not put forth my hands to iniquity. I seek the peace of Jerusalem, and I prosper because I love her. Peace and tranquility are within my walls; prosperity and blessings are within my home.

I am blessed because I reverence the Lord. I walk in His ways. I eat the labor of my hands. It is well with me now. I know that my tabernacle shall be in peace. All these blessings are coming upon me now, and are overtaking me because I obeyed the voice of the Lord, my God. Blessed am I in the city and on my job. Blessed is the fruit of my body, and of my ground, and the works of my hands. Blessed am I when I come in, and blessed am I when I go out.

The Lord causes the enemies that rise up against me to be smitten before my face; they shall come out against me one way, but flee before me seven ways. The Lord commands His blessing upon me now in my storehouses and in all that I set my hands to do. The Lord blesses me in the land that He has given me. All the people of the Earth see that I am called by the name of the Lord, and they shall be afraid of me. The Lord makes me plenteous in goods. The Lord opens unto me His good treasure. He opens the Heavens to give rain unto my land in His season, and He blesses all the works of my hands. I lend unto many nations, and I borrow from no one. I owe no man. I love freely because the Holy Ghost who is given unto me sheds the love of God in my heart. The Lord makes me the head and not the tail, and I am always above and never beneath. I am a saint of the Lord, and I give reverence to Him. I have no wants because I reverence and fear Him.

Blessed be the God of my salvation, who loads me daily with the blessings of His goodness. The Lord gives me that which is good, and my land yields her increase. God satisfies my mouth with good things so that my youth is renewed like that of the eagle. Though my beginning was small, yet my latter end will greatly increase. The young lions do lack and suffer hunger, but I seek the Lord and shall not want any good thing. I am a child of God. I am the redeemed of the Lord, and whatsoever I say is so. I cannot be denied. I have whatever                 I                 say.

# Prayer for Business

*Deuteronomy 28:8*
*The Lord will command the blessing on You in Your*
*storehouses and in all to which You set Your hand.*

1. Heavenly Father, I thank You for Your manifold blessings in my life.
2. I thank You for giving me an inheritance with Your Son, Jesus, who is Lord of all and Heir of all things.
3. I am mindful of the fact that You bless and favor all that I touch. My business is blessed.
4. I commit my business into Your hand. Holy Spirit, I invite You to become my Partner in this business.
5. I declare that people will come into my business before they will go anywhere else, because I am the head and not the tail. My business shines as a city set on a hill, because I am here, and my light of eternal life shines as a city set on a hill. People will be drawn to my business because the presence of God says, "Welcome." I am favored of the Lord.
6. I release a good report about my business; its name, location, products, and online services are blessed. I declare excellence in my products, my destiny helpers, workers, and financial partners, in Jesus' name.
7. I declare a good report concerning me and my

business. The good report of my business will echo from the mouths of others. Patrons will tell their friends how excellent my business is.

8. I declare that I will receive $_____ per month income through this business, in Jesus' name. I shall have what I say to the glory of the Father.

9. I ask that You help me in all business decisions, transactions, sales, purchases, contracts, and deals for the utmost profit.

10. I ask You to help me hire hard-working, faithful, and honest employees.

11. I ask, Lord, for Your blessings upon this business. It will experience phenomenal growth in volume, sales, customers, and profit.

12. I call forth finances to flow into my business from the north, south, east, and west. Maximize my business's growth, potential, and opportunities.

13. I thank You that Your thoughts are good towards me. I have thoughts of peace (and not evil), prosperity and health, and an expected end.

14. I choose to pray God-sized prayers.

I thank You, O God, that hears and answers prayers. I ask for all of these things to be done in the precious name of Jesus Christ. Amen.

## SCRIPTURAL REFERENCES

| Genesis 12:2 | I will bless you And make your name great; And you shall be a blessing. |
|---|---|

| Deuteronomy 30:9 | The Lord, your God, will make you abound in all the work of your hand, in the [a]fruit of your body, in the increase of your livestock, and in the produce of your land for good. For the Lord will again rejoice over you for good as He rejoiced over your fathers. |
| --- | --- |
| Proverbs 8:21 | That I may cause those who love me to inherit wealth, That I may fill their treasuries. |
| Psalm 107:23 | Those who go down to the sea in ships, Who do business on great waters, They see the works of the Lord, And His wonders in the deep. |
| Proverbs 22:29 | Do you see a man who [excels in his work? He will stand before kings; He will not stand before unknown men. |

# PRAYERS OF WISDOM AND GUIDANCE

*James 1:5*
*If any of you lacks wisdom, let him ask of God, who gives to all liberally and without reproach, and it will be given to him.*

1. Mighty God, I thank You because You are the same yesterday, today and forever.
2. Lord, You are infinite, beyond measurement, and You are all-powerful.
3. You are good and You are the embodiment of perfect goodness.
4. You are kind, loving to Your people, and full of favor towards all of creation.
5. In Christ Jesus are hidden all the treasures of wisdom and knowledge, all of which are my portion
6. You are able to repeat the biographies of the great men and heroes of faith.
7. I'm praying that You give me a wise and understanding heart as You gave to Solomon.
8. You are doing something new in me. You're releasing great wisdom, insight and hindsight upon me.
9. Give me wisdom that is pure and holy that I may know how to speak, act, and live.
10. Let wisdom flow like a river that cannot be held back or dried up, in the name of Jesus.
11. Teach me how to walk wisely, talk wisely, live wisely

and act wisely.

12. Help me to guard my mind against errors, my heart against bad thoughts, and my life against evil actions.

13. Release supernatural wisdom to me to go through open doors of favor. Allow me to be able to distinguish the timing of what is being released through Your divine access.

14. Rearrange and reshape in this end-time movement.

15. Bring forth purity and strengthening like never before to release the wisdom and counsel of the Lord upon the Earth.

16. Release and bring forth the greatest demonstrations of Your power and Your voice upon the Earth.

17. Father, You have all wisdom and do great mighty miracles. You performed miraculous signs and wonders in the land for Your people.

18. I am increasing in wisdom and statue, and in favor with God and man.

19. I thank You for the right thoughts and right words for every occasion in exhortation, counseling, comforting and encouragement.

## SCRIPTURAL REFERENCES

| | |
|---|---|
| Exodus 28:3 | So you shall speak to all who are gifted artisans, whom I have filled with the spirit of wisdom, that they may make Aaron's garments, to consecrate him, that he may minister to Me as priest. |
| Exodus 35:31 | And He has filled him with the Spirit of |

| | |
|---|---|
| | God, in wisdom and understanding, in knowledge and all manner of workmanship. |
| Exodus 36:1 | And Bezalel and Aholiab, and every gifted artisan in whom the Lord has put wisdom and understanding, to know how to do all manner of work for the service of the sanctuary. |
| Deuteronomy 34:9 | Now Joshua the son of Nun was full of the spirit of wisdom, for Moses had laid his hands on him; so the children of Israel heeded him, and did as the Lord had commanded Moses. |
| 1 Kings 3:12 | "See, I have given you a wise and understanding heart." |
| 1 Kings 3:28 | And all Israel heard of the judgment which the king had rendered; and they feared the king, for they saw that the wisdom of God was in him to administer justice. |
| 1 Kings 4:29 | And God gave Solomon wisdom and exceedingly great understanding, and largeness of heart like the sand on the seashore. Thus Solomon's wisdom excelled the wisdom of all the men of the East and all the wisdom of Egypt. |
| Proverbs 2:6 | For the Lord gives wisdom; From His mouth come knowledge and |

| | understanding; He stores up sound wisdom for the upright; He is a shield to those who walk uprightly. |
|---|---|
| Luke 2:40 | And the Child grew and became strong [a]in spirit, filled with wisdom; and the grace of God was upon Him. |
| Luke 2:52 | And Jesus increased in wisdom and stature, and in favor with God and men. |
| Proverbs 3:13 | Happy is the man who finds wisdom, And the man who gains understanding. |
| Proverbs 19:8 | He who gets [a]wisdom loves his own soul; He who keeps understanding will find good. |
| James 3:17 | But the wisdom that is from above is first pure, then peaceable, gentle, willing to yield, full of mercy and good fruits, without partiality and without hypocrisy. |

## Bible Verses about God's Guidance

| | |
|---|---|
| Psalms 25:4-5 | Show me your ways, Lord, teach me your paths. Guide me in your truth and teach me, for you are God my Savior, and my hope is in you all day long. |
| James 1:5 | If any of you lacks wisdom, you should ask God, who gives generously to all without finding fault, and it will be given to you. |

| Psalm 16:7-8 | I will praise the Lord, who counsels me; even at night my heart instructs me. I keep my eyes always on the Lord. With him at my right hand, I will not be shaken. |
|---|---|
| Proverbs 3:5-6 | Trust in the Lord with all your heart and lean not on your own understanding; in all your ways submit to him, and he will make your paths straight. |
| Psalms 32:8-9 | I will instruct you and teach you in the way you should go; I will counsel you with my loving eye on you. Do not be like the horse or the mule, which have no understanding but must be controlled by bit and bridle or they will not come to you. |
| John 16:13 | But when he, the Spirit of truth, comes, he will guide you into all the truth. He will not speak on his own; he will speak only what he hears, and he will tell you what is yet to come. |

# Prayer for Favor of the Lord

***Psalm 5:12***
***For You, O Lord, will bless the righteous; with favor you will surround him as with a shield.***

1. Dear Heavenly Father, I come to You, in the name of Jesus Christ.
2. I ask for favor with You and favor with all men. I ask for favor at home, favor at work, favor in the marketplace, favor with my children, favor with my spouse, and favor with my relatives.
3. Lord, grant me favor with the members of my fellowship, favor with my customers, favor with my employer.
4. Dear Jesus, grant me favor in litigation, temper justice with mercy, intervene in my case, grant me favor before the presiding judge and those who are in authority.
5. Lord, I need Your favor in the interview that is ahead of me and in the business negotiation, property, contract or deal that I am looking into.
6. May Your goodness and mercy follow me all the days of my life, O Lord, my God. In the name of Jesus. Amen.

## Favor Confessions

The Lord has granted me life and favor. His care preserves my spirit. My spirit is strong, and I have a sound mind. I have ordered my cause and I'm vindicated. I have divine influence in every situation. I am favored wherever I go. The Lord has blessed me. He encompasses me with favor as with a shield. I am satisfied with favor; I am full with the blessing of the Lord. I possess that which is mine. I walk in divine favor. I am in favor both with the Lord and with men. The Lord is the glory of my strength, and in His favor, my horn is exalted. The Lord is my defense, and the Holy One of Israel is my King. By His favor, I stand strong. I have the favor of the Lord, and I see the good of His chosen. I rejoice in the gladness of His nation and glory with His inheritance.

I love righteousness and hate wickedness; therefore, my God has anointed me with the oil of gladness above my companions.

The anointing of the Holy Ghost upon my life makes me glad and empowers me.

Honorable men and women are in my circle of influence. They will never come empty. They come with gifts. The rich among the people will seek my favor. They bring to me gold and silver. They will forget their own people and their father's house where I am concerned, and favor me above them. What is mine is finding its way to me now. I cannot be denied. The Lord is the health of my countenance and my

God. This is the portion of mine inheritance; He maintains my lot. The lines are fallen unto me in pleasant places; yes, I have a Godly heritage. I am precious in God's sight, and I am honorable.

I cannot walk in fear because God is with me. He brings my seed from the east and gathers me from the west. The north gives up and the south does not hold back that which is mine because the favor of the Lord is upon me. I am the redeemed of the Lord, and whatsoever I say is so. I cannot be denied. I have whatever I say. I am blessed. Amen.

## SCRIPTURAL REFERENCES

| | |
|---|---|
| Genesis 39:4 | So Joseph found favor in his sight, and served him. Then he made him overseer of his house, and all that he had he put under his authority. |
| Exodus 11:3 | And the Lord gave the people favor in the sight of the Egyptians. Moreover the man Moses was very great in the land of Egypt, in the sight of Pharaoh's servants and in the sight of the people. |
| Proverbs 3:3 | Let not mercy and truth forsake you; Bind them around your neck, Write them on the tablet of your heart, And so find favor and high esteem In the sight of God and man. |
| Daniel 1:9 | Now God had brought Daniel into the favor and [c]goodwill of the chief of the eunuchs. |

| Luke 2:52 | And Jesus increased in wisdom and stature, and in favor with God and men.⏻ |

# PRAYERS OF REVEALING OF SECRETS

## *Daniel 2:22*
*He reveals deep and secret things; He knows what is in the darkness, And light dwells with Him.*

1. I thank and praise Your glorious name for Your goodness and for Your tender mercies.
2. God, reveal the secrets concerning situations, circumstances, and motives, for nothing is hidden from You.
3. Unravel the whole mystery to me through dreams and visions of the night.
4. Lord restore my spiritual eyes, remove every veil that blurs my visions and dreams.
5. Father, reveal Your mind to me concerning this issue……….
6. Bring to light, O Lord, through visions, dreams and revelations, every plan of the enemy against me.
7. Lord, You use dreams and visions to give message and warnings to Your servants and prophets of old, even so, I pray that You will use this medium to communicate with me.
8. Show me strategies to overcome the obstacles of the enemy.
9. Make it clear to me what is holding me back in the spirit realm. Make my path shine as bright as the

morning sun. Your Word says that I should call to You and You would show me great and mighty things which I do not know.

10. Thank You for allowing me access to Your throne room. I praise You, Jehovah Rohi, because You know all and You see all.

11. You revealed the meaning of the king of Babylon's dream to Daniel, Your prophet, when he prayed; likewise Lord, I ask that You reveal the secret behind this matter, situation, problem and motives.

12. Lord, heal my spiritual blindness and give me clear and discerning spiritual sight that cannot be deceived.

13. Reveal potential dangers, disasters, fraud and mischief, so that I might pray and avert such from happening.

14. My entire life and destiny is in Your hands, and I know You can bring it all to pass.

15. Thank You for the answer to my prayers, in Jesus' name. Amen.

## SCRIPTURAL REFERENCES

| Daniel 2:28 | But there is a God in Heaven who reveals secrets, and He has made known to King Nebuchadnezzar what will be in the latter days. |
|---|---|
| Daniel 2:18 | That they might seek mercies from the God of Heaven concerning this secret...so the secret was revealed to Daniel in a night vision. So Daniel blessed the God of Heaven. |

| Daniel 2:47 | The king answered Daniel, and said, "Truly your God is the God of gods, the Lord of kings, and a revealer of secrets, since you could reveal this secret. |
| --- | --- |
| Ephesians 1:17 | That the God of our Lord, Jesus Christ, the Father of glory, may give to you the spirit of wisdom and revelation in the knowledge of Him, 18 the eyes of your [a]understanding being enlightened; that you may know what is the hope of His calling, what are the riches of the glory of His inheritance in the saints. |
| Psalm 44:21 | Would not God search this out? For He knows the secrets of the heart. |
| Matthew 10:26 | Therefore do not fear them. For there is nothing covered that will not be revealed, and hidden that will not be known. |
| 1 Corinthians 2:10 | But God has revealed them to us through His Spirit. For the Spirit searches all things, yes, the deep things of God. |
| Luke 8:17 | For nothing is secret that will not be revealed, nor anything hidden that will not be known and come to light.⏹ |

# PRAYERS FOR SINGLES

***Proverbs 18:22***
***He who finds a wife finds a good thing, and obtains favor
from the Lord.***

1. Father in Heaven, I humbly come before Your throne to thank You and to praise Your wonderful name for all Your goodness in my life. I posture my heart in Your presence, and touch You with my praise.

2. Lord, it is a deep desire of my heart to have a partner. I am laying this request at Your feet, knowing that You want me to have one.

3. Lord, I pray for a mate who is loving, kind, gentle and compassionate.

4. Lord, I pray for a mate who is responsible, industrious, a prayer warrior, a worshiper, an intercessor, one who has studied and who can show himself or herself approved unto You, a workman that need not to be ashamed, but rightly dividing the Word of Truth.

5. Lord, I want a mate who loves You as dearly as I do. A mate who would be my very best friend, who I can trust with my life—a co-laborer in the work of the Lord.

6. Lord, consider the pain of my lonely nights and of my intense longing and yearning, and help me.

7. Dear God, bring me in contact with the individual who is Your choice of a mate for me by Your divine

providence. Let it be love at first sight; a love that is stronger than death.

    8.  Lord, look upon Your servant and grant me the desires of my heart, for it is written "The desires of the hearts of the righteous shall be granted."

All these I ask and receive the answers to, even now by faith, in the name of Jesus Christ. Amen.

## SCRIPTURAL REFERENCES

| | |
|---|---|
| 1 Corinthians 7:2 | Nevertheless, because of sexual immorality, let each man have his own wife, and let each woman have her own husband. |
| Ecclesiastes 4:11 | Again, if two lie down together, they will keep warm; but how can one be warm alone? |
| Proverbs 19:14 | Houses and riches are an inheritance from fathers' but a prudent wife is from the Lord. |
| Proverbs 31:10 | Who can find a virtuous wife? For her worth is far above rubies. The heart of her husband safely trust her; so he will have no lack of gain. |
| Isaiah 34:16 | Search from the book of the Lord and read: Not one of these shall fail; not one shall lack her mate. For My mouth has commanded it, and His Spirit has gathered them. |
| Psalm 145:16 | You open Your hand and satisfy the desire of every living thing. Even desires for mates. |

| Proverbs 3:5-6 | Trust in the Lord with all your heart, and lean not on your own understanding; In all your ways acknowledge Him, and He shall direct your paths. |
|---|---|
| Psalm 37:4 | Delight yourself also in the Lord, and he shall give you the desires of your heart. |
| Proverbs 31:30 | Charm is deceitful and beauty is passing, but a woman who fears the Lord, she shall be praised. |

# INTERCESSION FOR SINGLES

1. Father in Heaven, allow them to feel Your anointing in every area of their lives. It is written, "The single was to seek to please You...the unmarried woman careth for the things of the world." Cause the single women to know their value, give them a mind to fall in love with You, and to stay the course so that they can reach the destiny You have already laid out for them.

2. I bind all distractions that the enemy would set before them. I break every curse from over their lives, in Jesus' name. Help them to be worshipers, intercessors, and victorious beings. Help them to walk in liberty, wherewith You have made them free.

3. I bind all annoyances, fear of being alone, and fear of never being married. I bind the enemy that would torment their minds about marriage.

4. I break the assignment of lust and perversion over them now. Lord, fill the voids in their lives and complete them. You will never leave them nor forsake them.

5. I loose the mind of Christ. Stir within them a praying and a fasting spirit. Let Your glory rest upon their countenance. Beautify their meekness with salvation. Teach them how to delight themselves in You, and grant them their hearts' desire. Help them to be content until the appointed time. Jesus, You are an Enabler of the Saints.

6. I bind all loneliness, rejection, doubt, walls, unbelief, self-will, discouragement, jealousy, envy and strife, in Jesus' name.

7. Protect them from all deceptions.

8. Bless them with witty inventions and businesses. Supply their needs, according to Your riches. I loose the spirit of wealth, in the name of Jesus.

9. Prepare them for marriage, if it be Your will. Your will be done, and Your Will will supersede all other wills, in Jesus' name. Amen.

# PRAYERS FOR MARRIAGE

**Proverb 5:18-19**
*Let your fountain be blessed, and rejoice with the wife of your youth. As a loving deer and a graceful doe, let her breasts satisfy you at all times; and always be delighted with her love.*

1. Great and Mighty God, I thank You for my spouse and the family You have given me.
2. I pray that I will find love and security in the arms of my spouse.
3. You ordained marriage before the Church.
4. Bless our marriage. Bind us together with cords of love that cannot be broken.
5. Empower us by Your Spirit to be the best loving, caring couple. May we have a healthy marriage.
6. Enrich our time of intimacy with a strong physical, emotional and spiritual bonding, and bless us with fulfillment. Invigorate and intensify our love and desires for each other.
7. I place this marriage on the foundation of the Word of God. I commit my marriage to the integrity, character and loyalty of the Kingdom of God, along with His purpose and will for us.
8. May your love for each other continue to grow stronger day by day.

9. Help us to avoid petty arguments and little annoyances that often sour relationships.

10. Take out all contention, strife, control, Ahab spirits and Jezebel spirits {footsteps}, and help us to submit to one another.

11. We bind comparison to other women/men, ungodly memory recall of the past, unhappiness, the feeling of being stuck, repressed emotions, regrets, sorrow, and all abuse, whether mental or physical. Deliver our soul.

12. Your Word says, "Two are better than one; because they have a good reward for their labor" (Ecclesiastes 4:9).

13. Give us patience and forbearance that we might be able to forgive and forget whenever we offend each other.

14. Protect us from outside negative influences from in-laws, friends and the devil.

15. May we, in all things, seek the interest and welfare of one other.

16. May he say in the true spirit of love, "You have captured my heart. My sister, my spouse; you have ravished my heart with one look of your eyes" (Song of Solomon 4:9).

17. Your lips, O my spouse, drip as the honeycomb; honey and milk are under your tongue (Song of Solomon 4:11).

18. May she say in true spirit of love, "I am my beloved's, and his desire is toward me" (Song of Solomon 7:10).

19. God, look on every helpmate and breathe upon them in a special way. Crown her head with wisdom, in the name of Jesus, to be a wise woman, for Your Word says, "Every wise woman builds her house: but the foolish plucks it down with her hands" (Proverbs 14:1).

20. Thank You, Lord, that You said, "Therefore shall a man leave his father and his mother, and shall cleave unto his wife: and they shall be one flesh" (Genesis 2:24).

21. May we set each other as a seal upon our hearts. For love is as strong as death; many waters cannot quench love, nor can the floods drown it.

22. Remove jealousy far from our hearts, for jealousy is as cruel as the grave. Its flames are flames of fire that consume everything in its path.

23. Give us absolute confidence and trust in each other. May the devil never tempt us to look at another or commit infidelity.

24. Take my marriage and mold it according to Your will that it may be a witness and a testimony of the love of Christ Jesus for His Church, the Bride and Bride-Groom.

25. May we cherish, respect and honor each other. Help us to keep our vows and renew them daily.

26. Your Word says for the husband to love his wife as Christ loves the church.

27. Fill every void.

28. Father, teach the husband how to sacrifice, love, endure, correct, work, be an example, show

compassion, be kind, be gentle (but not without strength), and most of all, to lay down his life, desires and will for his Father, even as You have for the church body.

29. Help him to be a friend to his wife.

30. Give wisdom, for wisdom is the principal thing.

31. I loose a praying marriage.

32. Help them to be slow to speak and quick to listen.

33. Help her to be a virtuous woman, and help him to be a mighty man of valor. Help them to both follow after righteousness and mercy, in the name of Jesus.

34. We bind pride, ego, anger, and lies that have been spoken in the ear. We bind seduction in the walk, talk and actions of any woman/man who has pulled on, convinced or deceived married individuals, in Jesus' name.

35. Lord, Your Word says, "By humility and the fear of the Lord are riches, and honor, and life" (Proverbs 22:4).

36. Help the wife and husband to become great intercessors, selfless in the things of God.

37. Teach the husband how to pray; teach him how to fight the good fight of faith for his family.

38. Lord, work miracles on their behalf.

39. Whatever their hands find to do, let them be busy and not idle.

40. We break every curse back a thousand generations on the mother's side and the father's side.

41. I pray that our romance will maintain the level of when we first met, and increase as the days pass, keeping our sex life and organs healthy ad vibrant.
42. May we never speak harshly to each other or allow anger to rule our minds.
43. May our love for each other dwell in us and reign in us till death do us apart. Amen.
44. Give us hope and joy in all things, and let us be an example of a victorious, blessed and successful couple, in the name of Jesus.
45. I place a blood shield and blood wall around our marriage, in Jesus' name.
46. I apply the blood of Jesus to our minds.
47. Bless this marriage and prosper it with health, wealth, wisdom and love for Your glory, in Jesus' name.

Thank You for listening to our prayers and answering them. For all these and much more we pray, in the precious name of Jesus Christ. Amen.

## SCRIPTURAL REFERENCES

| | |
|---|---|
| Genesis 2:24 | Therefore a man shall leave his father and mother and be joined to his wife, and they shall become one flesh. |
| Proverb 12:4 | An excellent wife is the crown of her husband, but she who causes shame is like rottenness in his bones. |
| Proverb | He who finds a wife finds a good thing, and |

| 18:22 | obtains favor from the Lord. |
|---|---|
| Ecclesiastes 9:9 | Live joyfully with the wife whom you love all the days of your vain life... |
| Hebrew 13:4 | Marriage is honorable among all, and the bed undefiled... |
| Colossians 3:18 | Wives, submit to your own husbands, as it fitting in the Lord. |
| Colossians 3:19 | Husbands, love your wives and do not be bitter toward them. |
| Ephesians 5:22 | Wives, submit to your own husbands, as to the Lord. For the husband is head of the wife, as also Christ is head of the church; and He is the Savior of the body. |
| Ephesians 5:24 | Therefore, just as the church is subject to Christ, so let the wives be to their own husbands in everything. |
| Ephesians 5:25 | Husbands, love your wives, just a Christ also loved the church and gave Himself for her. |
| Ephesians 5:28 | So husbands ought to love their own wives as their own bodies; he who loves his wife loves himself. |

# Prayers for Children and Youth

*Isaiah 8:18*
*Here am I and the children who the Lord has given me!*
*We are for signs and wonders in Israel.*

1. Almighty God, I want to thank You for the beautiful children (grandchildren, and great-grandchildren) that You have given me.
2. I pray for each one of them and speak Your blessings over their lives. I and the children that You have given me are for signs and wonders in this land.
3. Give me great love for my children. Help me not to provoke them to anger, lest they be discouraged.
4. I commit these children to Your hands. Take them Lord; they are Yours and Yours alone. Help them to make wise choices in every area and event of their lives.
5. Lord, draw these children into the light from darkness.
6. Cause them to see their sins and mourn. Lord Jesus, reveal Yourself to them, and help them to accept You as their Lord and Savior.
7. I pray that Your goodness and mercy will follow them all the days of their lives.
8. May they grow up in the fear of the Lord, and may their lives be enriched greatly with divine wisdom, knowledge and understanding.

9. I pray that Your angels will watch over them at all times and be their bodyguards.

10. I pray that they will grow up to become a pride and a blessing to our family, a pride to our society, and that they bring great honor and glory to Your name.

11. Keep them, O God, from bad influences. Keep them from drugs, alcohol, nicotine, all immoral behaviors, identity crises, and ungodly lifestyles. Let them love what You love and hate what You hate.

12. Set free those who are caught in the dreadful net of witchcraft and satanism. Wrestle them out of the grip and control of the devil, and help them to escape to safety in You.

13. Rescue those kids caught up in gangs, drug trafficking, sex trafficking, and violence. Cause them to lay down their weapons of hate, abstain from the life of lawlessness, and escape from the bonds of their oppressors.

14. Protect and safeguard their minds against the immoral filth on television, and the ungodly messages and lyrics of demonically inspired music.

15. Compel the rebellious, the careless, and the runaway to sit down and think. Holy Spirit, touch and soften their calloused and hardened hearts.

16. Shield them from peer pressure; help them to avoid self-destructive behaviors, as well as self-defeating attitudes and actions.

17. Give them a heart of flesh and a humble and obedient spirit. Cause them to return home with a repentant

heart. Make them happy children who are wise, discrete and intelligent.

18. Keep them away from bad influences and companies.

19. Protect our youth; teach them abstinence, stop and restrain them from any occasion that might lead to unwanted pregnancies, O Lord, our Father.

20. Father, show them Your love wherever they feel rejected. Heal deep inner hurts caused by harsh and hateful words. Heal them from the effects of mental, emotional, and sexual abuse, including rape. Heal them from the effects and traumas caused by the system of this world.

21. Some are in great trouble; deliver them, I pray. Others are in great fear; drive the taunting spirit of fear far away from them.

22. Some are greatly depressed, and they are thinking of taking their own lives. Fill them with joy and peace from Your throne.

23. Let Your angels be their bodyguards.

24. I come against the spirits of rebellion and waywardness. Stay away from my children. I bind and cast such spirits from them in Jesus' name.

25. Lord, have mercy on these children and grant each one of them blessings from on high. Keep them in much prayer. Hold them by their hands, and lead them on the path of truth and righteousness.

26. Guide and direct their steps on the path of truth and righteousness. Hold them by Your hands, and lead

them along the path of life with wisdom and discretion.

27. May our daughters become the foundations of many generations.

28. May our daughters be polished, and may they have the spirit of excellence over them, in the name of Jesus.

29. Our daughters will not struggle to get married, and no men will take advantage of them.

30. Our sons will be prepared adequately for their wives. I loose the spirit of obedience and loyalty into them.

31. My sons and daughters will not be involved with anyone who will become a liability to them, and they will not depend on their spouses to survive.

32. They shall be men who will be in charge of situations in their homes, and nothing will offend them.

33. My children shall walk in God's divine order. They shall be taught and retaught about the Lord, and their peace and tranquility shall be great, in the name of Jesus.

34. I declare shalom upon our offspring. Lord, make them dwell in safety.

35. I break every spirit of bitterness and anger from off our children, in the name of Jesus.

36. I bind the spirit of suicide and all suicidal tendencies, in the name of Jesus.

37. Our sons shall be mighty upon the Earth, whether bond or free.

38. My children are a heritage of the Lord and the fruit of the womb is our reward.
39. Let them be groomed in every way possible: mentally, spiritually, physically, emotionally, academically, geographically, financially, and globally.
40. May liberty and wholeness be their portion in the land of the living.
41. My children shall live long on the Earth and maximize their God-given potential in this lifetime.
42. I loose upon them the spirit of knowledge, the spirit of counsel, the spirit of wisdom, the spirit of understanding, the spirit of might, and the spirit of rulership, in the name of Jesus.
43. There shall not be any problems that they cannot solve.
44. Make them the head and not the tail. Put them on top and not beneath. Cause them to excel in all of their life-undertakings, O God.
45. Make them great leaders of tomorrow. Stir up creativity, gifts, talents, potentials and calling on the inside of them.
46. Establish them in peace and righteousness. May they never die young, but live out their days, even a hundred and twenty years plus, according to Your promise.
47. May their lives be a source of continual joy and praise to Your holy name.

## SCRIPTURAL REFERENCES

| | |
|---|---|
| Psalm 128:3 | Your wife shall be like a fruitful vine In the very heart of your house, Your children like olive plants All around your table. |
| Isaiah 54:13 | All your children shall be taught by the Lord, And great shall be the peace of your children. |
| Joel 2:28 | And it shall come to pass afterward That I will pour out My Spirit on all flesh; Your sons and your daughters shall prophesy, Your old men shall dream dreams, Your young men shall see visions. |
| Psalm 37:25 | I have been young, and now am old; Yet I have not seen the righteous forsaken, Nor his descendants begging bread. |
| Psalm 103:17 | But the mercy of the Lord is from everlasting to everlasting on those who fear Him, And His righteousness to children's children. |
| 1 Timothy 4:12 | Let no one despise your youth, but be an example to the believers in word, in conduct, in love, in spirit, in faith, in purity. |
| Ephesians 6:2 | Children, obey your parents in the Lord, for this is right. Honor your father and mother," which is the first commandment with promise: "That it may be well with you and you may live long on the earth. |
| Proverbs 3:11-12 | My son, do not despise the chastening of the Lord, Nor detest His correction; For whom |

| | the Lord loves He corrects, Just as a father the son in whom he delights. |
|---|---|
| Proverbs 13:24 | He who spares his rod hates his son, But he who loves him disciplines him promptly. |
| Proverbs 19:18 | Chasten your son while there is hope, and let not your soul spare for his crying. |
| Proverbs 20:20 | Whoever curses his father or his mother, His lamp will be put out in deep darkness. |
| Proverbs 22:6 | Train up a child in the way he should go, ]And when he is old he will not depart from it. |
| Proverbs 22:15 | Foolishness is bound up in the heart of a child; The rod of correction will drive it far from him. |
| Proverbs 23:13 | Do not withhold correction from a child, For if you beat him with a rod, he will not die. |
| Proverbs 23:14 | You shall beat him with a rod, And deliver his soul from hell. |
| Proverbs 29:15 | The rod and rebuke give wisdom, But a child left to himself brings shame to his mother. |
| Proverbs 29:17 | Correct your son, and he will give you rest; Yes, he will give delight to your soul. |
| Colossians 3:21 | Fathers, do not provide your children, lest they become discouraged. |

# PRAYERS AGAINST ORPHAN SPIRIT

1. Father in Heaven, bridge the gap, and as I draw close to You, You will draw close to me with no barriers, hindrances, or limitations.
2. I ask that every wall of anxiety, doubt, fear, unbelief, and pride that have been built up in my life come down.
3. Break the chains of the orphan spirit that is hindering me.
4. I put the ax to the root of the orphan spirit.
5. I plead the blood of Jesus upon myself, and I bind every spirit of orphanhood from my life.
6. I loose and release the Holy Spirit to hover over me to bring healing and deliverance.
7. I am separated from all false labels in my mind that evil people have placed upon me, in Jesus' name.
8. I bind the characteristics of the orphan spirit, unwantedness, trying to impress people, people-pleasers, an unbiblical view of what God thinks about me, focusing on the faults of those in authority, unteachable, building walls, needing recognition, a closed heart, opportunistic, an independent spirit, self-reliant attitude, pride, control, anger, disappointment, discouragement, pain, and loneliness of the moment, emotional damages, insecurity, inability to receive comfort, oppression, heaviness, lack of basic trust, fear, defiance, fighting,

PRESSING INTO POWERFUL PRAYER

manipulation, deception, faulty foundation, bondage, instability, free will, lack of trust, inability to receive discipline. Hebrews 12:6-8 reads, "For whom the Lord loves He chastens. And scourges every son whom He receives. If you endure chastening, God deals with you as with sons; for what son is there whom a father does not chasten? But if you are without chastening, of which all have become partakers, then you are illegitimate and not sons."

9.  Holy Spirit, guide and direct my friendships. "A man that hath friends must shew himself friendly" (Proverb 18:24).
10. I forgive those who walked away from me.
11. Lord, I ask that You forgive me for any blame, bitterness, or ungodly feelings that I have against others and myself, in Jesus' name.
12. Father, I repent and renounce any agreement with the orphan mindset.
13. I take authority over that mentality, in Jesus' name, and I break its hold over my mind.
14. Lord, You are my Father, my Daddy God, my Heavenly Father, my Eternal Father, and I pray that I will receive the spirit of adoption (Romans 8:15), and that I will call You, "Abba."
15. Lord, I pray that healing will come to every area of my heart.
16. I wipe away the scars that are in my heart from word curses that were placed on me throughout my life. They are all void, and have no effect on my life from this day forward.

17. Where my heart has become stony, I pray that You would make it a heart of flesh (Ezekiel 11:19).

18. Lord, I ask that You will bring committed spiritual fathers into my life to cover me in prayer, to give me direction, and to love me, in Jesus' name.

19. Lord God, forgive me for embracing the attitudes, actions, and heart of an orphan.

20. My heart and desire for me is to be a healthy part of a spiritual family.

21. I break all soul ties I have formed with an orphan spirit, in Jesus' name. I close every door the enemy had access to that gave him legal grounds in my life.

22. I bind my body, heart, and spirit to God's will and purpose for me, in Jesus' name.

23. Lord, I ask that You would heal my mind and my heart from the spirits of abandonment, rejection, and fatherlessness.

24. Lord, help me to pray for and support the spiritual fathers You have placed in my life.

25. Help me to model the attitude and heart that Jesus had towards You as He walked this Earth.

26. Lord, reveal to me all areas in my life that have been wounded.

27. Heal those areas and make me whole from the inside out.

28. Lord, I ask that You help me to forgive everyone who I looked up to as a spiritual father, leader, apostle, prophet, or mentor who wounded or failed me.

29. Lord, help me to commit to a church, be planted in a church and be submitted to a spiritual Father, in Jesus' name.
30. I thank You that I am Your son/daughter and that You have blessed me with an eternal inheritance of Your everlasting love. I receive Your love and forgiveness, and decree that I am accepted and part of the family of God.
31. I embrace my true self as beloved of the Lord in Your Kingdom and reign on Earth, for You and with You, in Jesus' name.
32. I am awakened to love. I believe and know that I am radically safe and settled in life, and I've found my home in Papa God, in Jesus' name. Amen.

## SCRIPTURAL REFERENCES

| | |
|---|---|
| John 14:18 | I will not leave you orphans; I will come to you. |
| Matthew 23:8 | Do not call anyone on earth your father; for One is your Father, He who is in heaven. |
| Psalm 68:5 | A father of the fatherless, and a defender of widows, is God in his holy habitation. |
| Psalm 146:9 | God relieves the fatherless and widow; but the way of the wicked He turns upside down. |
| Zephaniah 3:17 | The Lord your God is in your midst, a mighty one who will save; he will rejoice over you with gladness; he will quiet you by his love; |

he will exult over you with loud singing.

# Prayers Against Barreness

## Psalm 113:9
*He grants the barren woman a home, like a joyful mother of children.*

1. Great and Mighty God, I thank You for the gift of children, for You said to Adam to be fruitful and multiply.
2. I thank You, my Creator, for all the blessings You have given to me. I am grateful to You for granting me divine protection, provision, perfection and restoration.
3. Father God, I give You praise because You are worthy. There is none like You. You alone are God, the Most High. You reign supreme in my life and over all creation.
4. My Lord, I acknowledge that it is by Your grace that I am saved, blessed, fruitful, secure, prosperous and favored in all things.
5. It is written, "Children are the heritage from the Lord and the fruit of the womb as a reward from You."
6. It is written that I and my wife would be a fruitful vine by the side of our house, and our children like olive plants around our table.
7. Abba Father, You have healed the wombs in my family.

8. I ask that You will show us mercy and kindness, and touch our bodies just as You healed the household of Abimelech and they bore children.

9. You healed Sarah, Abraham's wife and she bore Isaac.

10. Father, cause me to laugh and remove my reproach from among men, in the name of Jesus.

11. Lord, as You can see, around our table has remained empty. We desire to have children around our table, just as You promised. Give us Godly children, O God.

12. In the Bible, You made the barren womb to keep house and to be a joyful mother of children.

13. The Word of God says, "Assuredly, I say to you, whatever you bind on earth will be bound in heaven, and whatever you loose on earth will be loosed in heaven" (Matthew 18:18).

14. Every demonic projection into my womb causing infertility, I uproot you in Jesus' name.

15. I break asunder every household wickedness refusing to release my fruitfulness.

16. Every household wickedness inflicting barrenness upon my marriage, either from my family's side or from my spouse's family, I bind and destroy you and your works, in the name of Jesus Christ.

17. Any satanic contraceptive the enemy has inserted into my reproductive organ, I command it to be uprooted and destroyed by fire, in Jesus' name.

18. I reject any and every medical result or report that claims that I cannot give birth naturally.

19. I silence every voice of barrenness speaking against my fruitfulness, in Jesus' name.
20. Every cause of barrenness, known and unknown, in my life and marriage, be destroyed by Holy Ghost fire, in Jesus' name.
21. When the barren Hannah cried to You, You heard her bitter cries, opened up her womb, and gave her children, among whom was Your great prophet and judge of Your people, Samuel.
22. Hear our cry, O God, and open up Your daughter's womb that she might bear children.
23. I shall conceive and give birth naturally in due season, in the name of Jesus Christ.
24. I thank You, Lord, for I now receive by faith the necessary empowerment to conceive. And according to the time of life, I shall bring forth a child for Your name and glory's sake. Amen.

## Scriptural References

| Genesis 18:14 | Is anything too hard for the Lord? At the appointed time I will return to you, according to the times of life, and Sarah shall have a son. |
|---|---|
| Deuteronomy 7:14 | You shall be blessed above all people, there shall not be a male or female barren among you or among your livestock. |
| Exodus 23:26 | No one shall suffer miscarriage or be |

barren in your land; I will fulfill the number of your days.

# PRAYERS FOR FAMILY

### Acts 16:31
*So they said, "Believe on the Lord Jesus Christ, and You will be saved, You and Your household."*

1. Dear God, I lift up my voice to You in prayer for all my relatives, both far and near.
2. Lord, bless my children, parents, brothers, sisters, uncles, aunts, cousins, nephews and in-laws.
3. You said if I believe in Jesus, You will make sure that my entire house would also be saved. I release my faith for the salvation of all my family members, in the name of the Father.
4. Except the Lord build the house, they labor in vain that build it: except the Lord keep the city, the watchman waketh but in vain.
5. Prosper them in every area of their lives. I speak Your blessings over each of their lives, both young and old.
6. I pray for a hedge of protection to be raised around them and their entire family.
7. Bring the careless and the godless among us to seek for mercy. Forgive and save their souls as they come. Establish them in faith.
8. I bind the spirit of slumber; I command their eyes that they should see, and ears that they should hear.
9. I bind the god of this world that has blinded their

minds, lest the light of the gospel of the glory of Christ, who is the image of God, should shine on them.

10. Heal any that are sick and make them well. Bring home the runaways and the renegades.

11. Tame the wild and the maniacs among us. Restrain them by Your mighty power.

12. Set those who are bound by addiction free, O God. Bid their addiction be gone! In Jesus' name.

13. Take cigarettes from between the fingers of those who smoke, and tobacco from between the teeth of those who chew.

14. Remove alcohol bottles from the lips of those who drink. Snatch the pipe and needle from those who are addicted to drugs.

15. Subdue their cravings for these mind-altering, judgment-impairing and life-destroying substances.

16. Cement and sweeten relationships between members of our families, O God, our Maker.

17. May we hear and celebrate the successes and achievements of each other.

18. Jesus, You said no man could come to You except the Father calls him.

19. Father, You are the God of the harvest. I ask that You call my family members into Your Kingdom now by the power of the Holy Spirit, in the name of Jesus.

20. Cause them to grow up in faith. I pray that they will always abound in the work of the Lord.

21. I believe that the north, the south, the east and the west have loosed them, and they are on their way to

be saved, delivered and set free, in Jesus' name. From eternity to eternity, You remain the same.

22. I stand in the gap, and I intercede for the forgiveness of the iniquities of my family.

23. I attack the power bases of the enemy. I send blood bombs and blood missiles against them, in the name of Jesus. My family shall be saved!

24. I make atonement as a member of the royal priesthood for the sins and iniquities of my family. You invite me to come and reason with You.

25. I ask for protection for my family from the plans and the attacks of the evil one, in the name of Jesus.

Father, thank You so much for this wonderful family You have given me, and I promise, in the name of Jesus, that as for me and my house, we will serve the Lord. Amen.

## SCRIPTURAL REFERENCES

| | |
|---|---|
| Psalm 103:17 | But the mercy of the Lord is from everlasting to everlasting On those who fear Him, And His righteousness to children's children. |
| Isaiah 44:3-4 | For I will pour water on him who is thirsty, And floods on the dry ground; I will pour My Spirit on your descendants, And My blessing on your offspring; Like willows by the watercourses.' |
| Psalm 102:28 | The children of Your servants will continue, And their descendants will be established |

before You."

## Family Prophetic Decrees

I pray that the hearts of the fathers be turned towards the children, and that the disobedient would be turned to the wisdom of the just—to make ready a people prepared for the Lord.

I intercede for the youth: that they would be strong in the Lord—a generation passionate for You, sold out and on fire for the Kingdom of God.

Protect them from all harm and deceit, and from all the works of the enemy, and let Jesus reign in them.

Let the spirit of Elijah be released in our states, cities, regions, and borders, in Jesus' name.

I decree family restoration, deliverance amongst the body of Christ. Let revival begin in my home.

I thank God that the Heavens are open, and I pray for restoration of all the things that the devil has stolen from me and my family, in Jesus' name. Amen.

# ELDERLY

***Isaiah 46:6***
***Even to your old age, I am He, and even to gray hairs I will***
***carry you! I have made, and I will bear; even I will carry,***
***and will deliver you.***

1. Blessed Savior, I thank You for how You have preserved my life and kept me alive till this age.
2. What shall I render to You, my God and my Maker, for Your great benefits and blessings from my youth till now?
3. I praise Your holy name for You have never left nor forsaken me.
4. I thank You for crowning my head with wisdom as I trained my children and grandchildren to be wonderful citizens and to be God-fearing citizens in our society.
5. You said that You would let nothing slip upon Your beloved. Show me the enemy afar off in my bloodline.
6. Hold my mind as You expose the enemy in my children at all times. I break every inherited curse and fear of training, correcting, teaching, loving and having natural affection, in Jesus' name.
7. Take out all frustrations, selfishness, and at times, feelings of loneliness in the rearing of my children.
8. Supply every need mentally, emotionally, physically, and financially, in Jesus Name.

9. You have always been by my side through the thick and the thin of life. You have walked by my side through the valley of the shadow of death. Your Spirit and Your angels have comforted and strengthened me.

| SCRIPTURAL REFERENCES | |
|---|---|
| Psalm 37:25 | I have been young, and now am old; Yet I have not seen the righteous forsaken, nor his descendants begging bread. |
| Psalm 121:7-8 | The Lord shall preserve you from all evil; He shall preserve your soul. The Lord shall preserve your going out and your coming in. From this time froth, and even forever more. |

# Confidence and Hope

*Psalm 33:18*
*Behold, the eye of the Lord is on those who fear Him, on those who hope in His mercy.*

1. Beloved Father, I come humbly before Your throne now to offer my prayer for mercy before You.
2. As the old hymn says, "My hope is built on nothing less than Jesus' blood and righteousness. I dare not trust the sweetest frame, but wholly lean on Jesus' name."
3. I have none in whom I can fully trust, none who can help me at the proper time with my needs, but only You, my God.
4. You are my Trust and Confidence, my Comforter, in all things.
5. I look therefore to You, my God, the Father of mercies, and in You, I put my hope.
6. You are all my desire; therefore, I earnestly pray to You and will continually hope in Your mercy and grace.
7. Lord, You are my only confidence and hope. Do not disappoint me of my hope in You. Perfect everything that concerns me, and guarantee my well-being, in Jesus' name.
8. My faith smiles when the problem is hopeless.
9. Let hope arise, and let it not be delayed any longer.

10. For as a servant looks unto his master and a handmaid looks unto her mistress, so I look unto You for my help.

11. As a baby clings to her mother, so I cling to You, my God and my Great Provider.

12. In the words of the Psalmist, "My eyes look up to the hills from whence comes my help." So Lord, my eyes look to Your throne, from whence comes my blessings.

13. Remember Your Word to Your servant, upon which You have caused me to hope.

14. My faith is in You, and it tells me that You are able.

15. You are our Healer and Helper, and we will hope in You.

16. I am drinking out of the river of God's pleasures, and I will marinate in His goodness and hope.

# PRAYERS FOR DELIVERANCE

*Isaiah 49:25*
*Even the captives of the mighty shall be taken away, And the prey of the terrible be delivered; For I will contend with him who contends with You, And I will save Your children.*

1. Father God, in the name of Jesus, I thank You for the redemptive work of Christ that took place on the cross.

2. I proclaim that Jesus Christ is Lord and Savior of my life, and I hereby pledge my allegiance to Christ's lordship over my life.

3. I am a child of the Most High, a child of the Light and a drinker of the Eternal River.

4. I am a seer of things to come, and I am fearless against the darkness.

5. I am a history maker, restorer of the break of love, and I am cloaked with humility.

6. Satan, I hereby renounce my allegiance to you, either directly or indirectly. I break all ties, oaths, covenants, vows, agreements that I have made or entered with you, either knowingly or unknowingly, in the name of Jesus.

7. Satan, if I owe you anything, I pay you now with the blood of Jesus Christ which was shed as a ransom for my freedom from your evil powers on the cross.

8.  I now command you, Satan, to get out of my life, my family and my business. I hereby burn and destroy all objects, paraphernalia, and regalia (if any) that pertain to your wicked practices.

9.  I break every inherited curse off of my life, and I command those spirits to loose and leave me, in Jesus' name.

10. I break off from my life every curse, spell, hex and every diabolical manipulation of the devil against me. The horse and its rider, He has thrown into the sea!

11. Lord Jesus, deliver me from all demonic possession, obsession, oppression, harassment and nightmares. Deliver me from every womb of darkness. Cause them to stop permanently, in Your precious name. Amen.

12. I render the power and the weapons of the enemy against my life powerless. For any weapon formed against me shall not prosper, in Jesus' name.

13. I bind all demonic forces on assignment against my life. I paralyze all their activities and frustrate all their efforts to do me harm, in Jesus' name. Amen.

14. I command every corruptible seed that has been imparted in me from any of those spirits to wither and die.

15. I will not allow you to root in me!

16. I pull you out by the roots, destroy your seeds, and command you to go!

17. Cause my tongue to build up and edify with wisdom, knowledge, and encouraging words.

18. Grant me the tongue of the learned.

19. Grant me a tongue of love, purity and healing.

20. Bridle my tongue for Your glory, and allow living water to flow from my mouth, putting out all fires from the evil one and nullifying his deadly poison.

21. Deliver me from any cockatrice spirit, gossiping, and backstabbing. Set me free!

22. I decree my mouth is the altar for sacrifice of praise, worship and the sword of the Spirit.

23. Grant my mouth to be a ready writer of dimensional revelation and declaration of strategy, warnings, encouragement, love and the deep things of God.

24. Father, I thank You that You're downloading, by the Holy Spirit, specific instructions to me in every situation.

25. Jesus, I thank You that Heaven will back what I declare in the Earth through the Kingdom of God by the Holy Spirit. So, I operate my authority in this prayer, according to what Heaven has ordained.

26. I choose this day life, forgiveness, and joy to proceed from my mouth.

27. Send Your angels to pursue and overthrow the evil king and warlocks wherever and whenever they gather together to do me harm.

28. I raise a hedge of protection around myself, my loved ones, both far and near, and all of my possessions. I cover all with the blood of Jesus.

29. Arise O Lord, and let all my enemies be scattered. Put them in great fear that they might believe in Your name.

30. Lord, I pronounce and declare that Satan's weapons are nullified against me, and I claim my peace, my righteousness, my security and my triumph over opposition.

31. Thank You, Lord, for delivering my soul from the jaws of death and destruction. Amen.

## SCRIPTURAL REFERENCES

| | |
|---|---|
| Joel 2:32 | And it shall come to pass that whoever calls on the name of the Lord shall be saved. For in Mount Zion and in Jerusalem there shall be deliverance. |
| Psalm 91:3 | Surely He shall deliver you from the snare of the fowler and from the perilous pestilence. |
| Jeremiah 15:21 | I will deliver you from the hand of the wicked, and I will redeem you from the grip of the terrible. |
| Psalm 107:6 | Then they cried out to the Lord in their trouble, and He delivered them out of their distresses. |
| Exodus 15:6 | Your right hand, O Lord, has become glorious in power; Your right hand, O Lord, has dashed the enemy in pieces. And in the greatness of Your excellence You have overthrown those who rose against You; You sent forth Your wrath; It consumed them like stubble. |
| 1 John 3:8 | For this purpose the Son of God was |

manifested, that He might destroy the works of the devil.

# Prayers for Trouble

*Psalm 91:15*
*He shall call upon Me, and I will answer him; I will be with him in trouble; I will deliver him and honor him. With long life I will satisfy him, and show him my salvation.*

1. Great and Mighty God, blessed be Your name forever and ever.
2. You said to call upon You in the day of trouble, and You will deliver me.
3. And now, dear Jesus, what shall I say? Send me help from the sanctuary, and grant me support and strength from Zion. Come and deliver me from this trouble.
4. Give me courage and patience in this time of need, O Lord, my Savior. Help me to endure it. Do not allow me to lose my mind or my faith, for my trust is in You alone.
5. Let Your powerful hand suppress and lessen the effects of this trouble, so that I do not completely sink under it, as You have so often done for me in the past.
6. For if the Lord be for me, You are more than the whole world against me.
7. Thank You, Lord, for I know that all things work together for the good of those who love You and called according to Your purpose. Even so, I believe

this trouble will work out for my good, in Jesus name. Amen.

## SCRIPTURAL REFERENCES

| Psalm 107:13 | Then they cried out to the Lord in their trouble, And He saved them out of their distresses. |
|---|---|
| Psalm 31:4 | Pull me out of the net which they have secretly laid for me, For You are my strength. |

# Prayer Against Deception and Lies

Almighty God, have mercy on me and allow Your grace to abound in my life. I ask You to please search me thoroughly and remove all of the demonic spirits that are attached to me, or that are residing in me, in Jesus' name. I understand that this Earth is ruled by deception through Satan's kingdom, and this deception is caused by delusion, compromise, confusion, smokescreens, bondage, fear, and the false doctrines of seductive devils.

I declare my freedom. I shall be free from all lies, fables, plagiarism, fear, the lust of the flesh, and the pride of life that causes me to sow into the flesh and reap corruption, opening doors to the demonic presences and influences in my life.

I repent from any association, agreement, or approval with these foul spirits of deception, false doctrines, lust, worldliness, and fear, in Jesus' name.

I take my God-given authority, and I command all seducing spirits of deception, strong delusion, confusion, compromise, complacency, laziness, legalism, manipulation, lukewarmness, and fear to leave my spirit, soul, mind, body, health, finances, family, relationships, business, and projects, according to the will and Word of God. I cast you spirits out, and I command you to find your entrance and exit and go to the pit, in Jesus' mighty name.

Lord, grant me eyes to see, ears to hear, and a pure heart to follow and obey You. Guide me in the path of righteousness and truth, manifesting Your Word, power, and favor all the days of my life. Allow me to be a witness to Your love, power, and truth, bringing glory to Your name while I maintain my breath on this side, in Jesus' name. Amen.

# Prayers of Freedom from Witchcraft and Unnecessary Warfare

Freedom has become elusive to many people. In fact, humanity has been roaming around in the darkness of witchcraft and bondage, without any way out. But the good message for you is that there is hope. You can be among the candidates who have been qualified through the blood of Jesus for total emancipation from bondage, satanism and witchcraft.

## What is Freedom?

Freedom means liberation or release from satanic and ungodly bondage or unfavorable situations. When this happens, an old era passes away and gives way to a better one. In other words, slavery is turned to liberty and freedom. That is why you need to pay serious attention and learn how to gain complete freedom from the shackles of bondage.

## The Spirit of Witchcraft

In 2 Kings 9:22, the author says, "And it came to pass, when Joram saw Jehu that he said, is it peace, Jehu? And he answered, what peace, so long as the whoredoms of thy mother Jazebel and her witchcrafts are so many?"

The spirit of witchcraft is very wicked and deadly; you must strive hard through aggressive prayers to be set free from the bondage of witchcraft.

You can be empowered to defeat the enemies of freedom. Very many people today have been held spellbound and confused by the powers that put people in the bondage and torments of witchcraft. This is why you must have the right attitude to defeat the enemies of freedom.

1. Lord, I acknowledge You as Creator and Overseer of all the universe and eternity through Christ Jesus.
2. I take hold of the horns of the altar. I return to the sender every satanic missile aimed at me. I repel every satanic maneuver against me, in the name of Jesus.
3. I know nothing is hidden from Your sight. As Your servant and covenant solider in Christ, I use the authority, power, and dominion You have granted to me against all powers of darkness and witchcraft. I am armed and dangerous, and I am a third-dimension warrior, in Jesus' name.
4. I bind, blind, mute, and deafen all powers of darkness that have been assigned to me, my family, health, finances, projects, jobs, businesses, ministries, possessions, territories, and destiny, in Jesus' name.
5. I break and loose myself from all witchcraft, sorcery, spells, and curses that have been inherited, self-

imposed, and spoken against me, in the name of Jesus. The curse causeless shall not come.

6. I repent for opening doors to witchcraft spirits through my involvement or compliance with accursed video games, television shows, music, Ouija boards, tarot cards, mediums, horoscopes, palm reading, occultism, martial arts rooted in Eastern religions, new age yoga, hypnosis, drugs, necromancy (praying to the dead), psychics, spiritualists, fortune cookies, witchcraft movies, witchcraft books, seances, abortion, false religions, sexual perversion, tattoos, pagan rituals, cutting, intrusive piercing, and all other practices of witchcraft, including those that I can't remember or am unaware of. I repent for myself and my family line. I break every hold in my life and in my family's life, and I cast these spirits and their curses back to the pit, in Jesus' name.

7. I come against the forces of witchcraft. I bring down every satanic manifestation, operation, resistance, intimidation, manipulation, domination, exploitation, setback, disappointment, and harassment. I take authority over and I bind every charismatic witchcraft prayer, curse, spell, and every non-scriptural demonic claim upon my life, in the name of Jesus. I cancel and reverse every negative word sent out against my progress right now. I bind death in every form, and every satanic prediction through the power of the blood of Jesus. I bind all satanic calculations and monitoring spirits. I uproot and destroy any

assignment of the enemy that has been released to hinder God's prophetic purposes for my life, in the mighty name of Jesus.

8.  I invoke the blood of Jesus against every enchantment and curse sent out against me. Father, You said in Your Word that whatever I bind on Earth shall be bound in Heaven, and whatever I loose on Earth shall be loosed in Heaven. I loose the blood of Jesus against the forces of evil, in the name of Jesus. I bind the curse of setbacks, in the name of Jesus.

9.  Father, I thank You for setting me free from every power of witchcraft and unnecessary warfare, in Jesus' name.

10. Every pillar of witchcraft mounted against me, fall and shatter, in the mighty name of Jesus.

11. Every foundational witchcraft bondage, die by fire, in the name of Jesus.

12. Every witchcraft tree caging my blessings, thunder of God, strike them, in the mighty name of Jesus.

13. Every witchcraft food in my system, be consumed by fire, in the name of Jesus.

14. Marine witchcraft, listen to me now! Die the death of Goliath, in Jesus' name.

15. The voice that called forth Lazarus, call forth my dead blessings, in Jesus' name.

16. Stubborn witchcraft, listen to me, die the death of Pharaoh, in Jesus' name.

17. Any capture from my life by witchcraft, I capture you back, in Jesus' name.

18. You witchcraft power, carry your evil load, in Jesus' name.
19. I command every power of the grave and death to release my blessings, in Jesus' name.
20. Every witchcraft power that is designed to keep me from prospering, die, in the name of Jesus.
21. Oh Lord, let the teeth of the enemy over my life break, in the name of Jesus.
22. I render every aggressive altar impotent, in the name of Jesus.
23. Oh Lord, my God, let the covenant with the Earth against my life be broken, in the name of Jesus.
24. Every evil altar erected against me, be disgraced, in the name of Jesus.
25. Oh Lord, my God, let every covenant with the sun against my life be broken, in Jesus' name.
26. Anything done against my life under a demonic anointing is nullified, in the mighty name of Jesus.
27. Let every covenant with the moon against my life be broken, in the name of Jesus.
28. I curse every local altar fashioned against me, in the name of Jesus.
29. Oh Lord, my God, let every covenant with the stars against my life be broken, in the name of Jesus.
30. Let the hammer of the Almighty God smash every witchcraft altar erected against me, in the name of Jesus.
31. Every bird of darkness working against my progress, fall down and die, in the name of Jesus.

32. No witch or wizard will thrive in my environment, in the name of Jesus.

33. Spirits of the water that are in a web of witchcraft against me, I judge you by fire, in the name of Jesus.

34. Queen of Heaven who is networked in witchcraft against me, I judge you by fire, in the name of Jesus.

35. Let the sun strike them by day and the moon by night, in the name of Jesus.

36. Oh Lord, my God, let the stars in their courses fight witches and wizards against my life, in the name of Jesus.

37. I have locked all the witchcraft buildings with the key of David, in the name of Jesus.

38. O God, arise and send Your whirlwind with great pain upon the head of witchcraft, in the name of Jesus.

39. O God, arise and subdue every witch, in the name of Jesus.

40. O God, arise and cause a stormy wind to fall upon the power of witches, in the name of Jesus.

41. Oh God, rise up and bring a day of disaster upon the heads of every witch that has sent out evil against my life and family, in the name of Jesus.

42. Every witchcraft spell and charm against my life is gone, in the name of Jesus.

43. I halt all witchcraft programs against my family, in Jesus' name.

44. Witches in the waters, I crush your powers, in the name of Jesus.

45. The witchcraft program for my destiny, I destroy you, in the name of Jesus.
46. Every witchcraft power assigned to turn my life into a dumping ground, I cast you down, in the name of Jesus.
47. Witchcraft powers assigned to be resurrected to bring distress to my life, die by fire, in the name of Jesus.
48. Every plan of the wizard game on my success has been destroyed, in the name of Jesus.
49. Every yoke that produced witchcraft to attack my life, be broken now, in Jesus' name.
50. Every painful pregnancy assigned to my progress by the powers of witchcraft, I interrupt and terminate you now, in Jesus' name.
51. My Father, I raise the blood-soaked banner of Jesus against any demonic or witchcraft junction where Your glory has been sacrificed, in the name of Jesus. O Lord, I raise an altar with the blood of Jesus against demonic curses, covenants, limitations, evil foundations and disorders in my destiny today. I command my destiny to be released by fire, in the name of Jesus. My Father, I raise an altar with the blood of Jesus against the altar of darkness militating against my health, in the name of Jesus.
52. Father, according to Your Word, preserve and keep me alive, and establish me upon the Earth. Father God, You have commanded Your loving-kindness in the daytime, and in the night, Your songs shall be with me. You will cause me to rejoice in You, for You are

the God of my life. You are God, my only safe haven. I praise Your name forever, in Jesus' name. Amen.

# CALL DOWN THE DESTRUCTIVE FIRE OF HOLY SPIRIT

It is not an easy thing to pull down satanic altars that were established in our fathers' houses. It is also not an easy thing to destroy witchcraft and evil altars, but as a child of God, you should be able to pull them down. When an altar is formed against a person or a family, certain spirits will be sent out against that person or that family, and they will be hindered.

The fire of God has the capacity to pull down the structures and altars erected in the father's and the mother's houses. The fire of God is the only formidable power that can shake altars and destroy their foundations. Every child of God must possess the raw fire of the Holy Ghost in order to destroy the satanic altars that are holding them in bondage.

With the fire of God, you can bind the strongman administering the evil altar. With the fire of God, you can command Heaven to open and rain fire on the altars of your enemies. With the fire of God in you, satanic altars cannot have access to penetrate into your life. When you have the strong fire of God, everything will fall into place for you. People who possess the fire of God always attract formidable demons, but in the end, they always reclaim total victory through Christ Jesus.

Today, very few people are willing to pay the price for lighting their altars with the fire of God. Ordering the fire of God on your altarpiece is the smartest thing to do. Sadly, many people don't have the power of God. This is why the devil always attacks them, despite the large Bibles that are under their pillows.

So when you have the fire of God to challenge the altars of Satan, the fire of God becomes the place of torment for the enemy. When you have the fire of God, no arrows from the wicked one can affect you. When you have the fire of God, God will protect you. If you do not have the fire of God, and you have defied the altars of Satan, the anger of the enemy will be against you.

The devil has drawn a line of battle against the victims. Sadly, most people do not or may not know the dangers of Satan's altars. That's why you see them go from one problem to a more difficult problem. When God activates His fire in you, you will become untouchable, and whatever evil that comes against you from the kingdom of darkness will be given to you, in the name of Jesus (Psalm 105:15).

1. Lord, send Your fire to destroy every evil altar and agenda fashioned against me, in the name of Jesus.
2. I arrest every evil bird fashioned against my breakthroughs, in the name of Jesus.

3.  Every evil priest ministering against me at the evil or witchcraft altar, receive the sword of God, in the name of Jesus.

4.  Let the thunder of God smite every evil priest working against me on the evil altar, and burn them to ashes, in the name of Jesus.

5.  Every bird of darkness on assignment against my destiny, be roasted, in the name of Jesus.

6.  I spray the blood of Jesus on the covens of witchcraft around me, in the name of Jesus.

7.  Let every satanic priest ministering against me at an evil altar fall down and die, in the name of Jesus.

8.  Any power assigned to use me as sacrifice, die, in the name of Jesus.

9.  Any hand that wants to retaliate or arrest me because of these prayer points I am praying, dry up and catch fire, in the name of Jesus.

10. Witchcraft altars set up against me, set your owner ablaze, in the name of Jesus.

11. Every stubborn evil altar priest, drink your own blood, in the name of Jesus.

12. I shall not be a candidate of the eaters of flesh and drinkers of blood, in the name of Jesus.

13. I possess my possessions stolen by witches and wizards, in the name of Jesus.

14. Holy Ghost fire, barricade my life from the rage of satanic birds, in the name of Jesus.

15. I withdraw my name from every witchcraft altar, in the name of Jesus.

16. I reject every bewitchment fashioned against my destiny by the birds of darkness, in the name of Jesus.
17. I withdraw my blessings and fire from every occultist altar, in the name of Jesus.
18. Any sickness assigned to overtake my life, catch fire and die, in the name of Jesus.
19. I release the fire of God to every evil altar demanding my family's blood, in Jesus' name.
20. I destroy every witch and wizard who is planning for my downfall by the fire of the Holy Ghost, in the name of Jesus.
21. Strange words assigned to trap me, scatter by fire, in the name of Jesus.
22. Every evil pot that arises to control my life, catch fire, in the name of Jesus.
23. I withdraw my prosperity from every satanic altar by fire, in the name of Jesus.
24. Everyone who has accepted witchcraft for my sake, be disgraced, in the name of Jesus.
25. My life, jump out of every inherited witchcraft cage, in the name of Jesus.
26. Anything buried to bury me, bury your owner, in the name of Jesus.
27. Holy Ghost fire, burn every evil altar in my generation, in Jesus' name.
28. I release my life and my destiny from every bondage of witchcraft and unnecessary warfare, in the name of Jesus.

29. Satan, my mouth is your obituary, in the name of Jesus. I am free from every satanic and witchcraft bondage, in the name of Jesus.

30. Christ has set me free from every evil bondage, and I am free indeed, in the name of Jesus. I am now sitting with Christ in Heavenly places! Therefore, my life, family, and ministry shall no longer be abased, debased, downtrodden, degraded, and subjected to shame, in the name of Jesus.

31. I shall be elevated in all ramifications of life, family, ministry, and destiny! Yes! I shall be elevated above witchcraft, spiritual dryness, poverty, evil attacks, occultist arrows, principalities, powers, sickness and disease, in the name of Jesus.

32. Throughout my lifetime, witches and wizards shall bow to me, demotion shall not be my portion, evil arrows and satanic agendas shall be destroyed, failure shall come under my feet, stagnation and retrogression shall be buried, and depression shall flee from me, in the name of Jesus.

33. God, I take back my authority, in the name of Jesus Christ, and I pray that You will destroy every organization, terrorist cell group, and government, both locally and globally, that dares to come against Your will or persecute Your people. Destroy every Ponzi scheme, drug trafficking, human trafficking, and weapon smuggling organization. Rain down fire on every pedophilic and sodomic organization, including

all high places where Satan's altars have been established, both locally and globally.

34. I call destructive fire down on all their gathering places, propaganda, websites, media, communications, storehouses and all financial support systems. I send confusion into the enemy's camp, and I sever all financial support, communications, websites, gatherings, agendas and any further operations, in Jesus' name.

35. I loose all those who have been taken captive to the deception of these demonic influences, in the name of Jesus. Amen.

# PRAYERS OF BREAKING GENERAL CURSES

***Galatians 3:13***
***Christ has redeemed us from the curse of the law, having become a curse for us for it is written, cursed is everyone who hands on a tree.***

The way to break curses is by repenting of any involvement that you have had with the enemy, his kingdom or his systems, and rebuke the demons in your life. You should also say something to the effect of:

"Father, I ask You first to forgive me for my sins and to cleanse me from any area where I have allowed the devil to enter into my life. I renounce all participation in the works of darkness. In the name of Jesus, I now take away every curse, and Father, please forgive the people who have spoken against me. I thank You that these curses are no longer working against me. In Jesus name, they are broken now by Your power, Almighty God. I cancel all evil that has been spoken or sent out against me, and I beg You to protect me and my family, according to Your Word in Psalm 91."

The Bible tells us in James 4:7: "Therefore surrender yourselves to God. Resist the devil and he will escape you."

If we believe that someone is cursing us, we should not send a curse to the one who sent it to us. We are not to return evil for evil, but overcome evil with good (Romans 12:21). Ask God to forgive you because often times, you don't know what you are doing. If we listen to the Word of God and allow the Holy Spirit to automatically reverse the curse, and if we speak well and pray for those who want to harm us, God will protect and bless us. We should also cite letters that promise us protection, such as Psalm 91.

Remember, the devil has fallen, and we have power over him, so we should not be afraid of him. When we use our authority over him in faith, he cannot harm us. We have power over all curses through our Lord, Jesus Christ.

"And He said to them, I saw Satan like lightning fall from heaven. Here I give you the strength to walk on snakes and scorpions, and above all the strength of the enemy: and nothing will hurt you" (Luke 10:18).

1. Heavenly Father, I thank You for sending Jesus to die on the cross of Calvary for my sins.
2. Jesus' blood has redeemed me from the curse of the law. I am blessed beyond measure.
3. Father, I plead the blood of Jesus over my life and the lives of my children.
4. In the name of Jesus, I put You in remembrance to Your Word, and I plead with You to blot out all

transgressions and iniquities that plague me and my family.

5. I break all generational curses from my parents and my great-great grandparents.

6. Hold not the sins of our fathers against us.

7. I break all illegal occupations and operations by familiar spirits in my family, in the name of Jesus.

8. In the name of the Lord, Jesus Christ, I take up the power of the cross, His death, His blood, His sacrifice, His resurrection, His life, His grave, His authority, His reign and His government. I release the judgment of the Lord, Jesus Christ, against all unclean powers, magic, black arts, and curses. I release the power of Jesus Christ against all counsel that is against me: written, spoken or carried out.

9. I release the blood of Jesus, the Son of God, against all kinds of blood sacrifices and cultures.

10. I take the sacrifice of Jesus Christ on the cross in opposition to all the sacred laws.

11. In the name and blood of Jesus Christ, I spoil every power, and I cast down every curse that comes to me by demonic ordinance or sacrifice.

12. In the name and blood of Jesus Christ, I break the power of every curse that came upon me through my family line.

13. In the name and blood of Jesus Christ, I break the power of every curse that has come to me through words.

14. In the name and in the blood of Jesus Christ, I break the power and hold of any curse that has come to me through occult practices.

15. In the name of Jesus Christ, I declare that every legal hold and every legal foundation of the enemy is broken, disarmed and destroyed. Satan can never attack me again with curses brought on by occult practices, sacrifices or rituals of any kind. By the blood of Jesus Christ, I am free. Thank You, Jesus, for setting me free. I now order these curses and affirmations completely disarmed and dismantled by the power and the blood of Jesus Christ, and in His name.

16. In the name of Jesus Christ, I command all demonic spirits who have accessed me through curses and rituals to be cut off and banished from me and my house, in the mighty name of the Lord, Jesus Christ.

17. Jesus, I ask You to send Your angels now to completely disarm all curses and dark arts sent out against me; disarm all their devices and destroy them. I ask Your angels to remove all evil spirits involved in these curses and tie them to Your feet for judgment.

18. Now, I claim every spiritual blessing my Heavenly Father has given me in Christ Jesus (Ephesians 1:3). I claim these blessings right here in place of any curse by the authority and power of the Lord, Jesus Christ, and in His name, so that these things can be fully accomplished now. Thank You, Lord. I honor and praise you.

19. I break and loose myself and my family from any vows I've made to any person, occult, psychic source, and any demons coming through my bloodline. I cancel all invitations made to unclean spirits.

20. Lord, I destroy all curses, sicknesses, diseases and impediments inherited from the bloodline of my family, in the mighty name of Jesus.

21. I renounce, break and loose myself and my family from all other religions, especially Roman Catholicism, Hinduism, Islam, Buddhism, Mormonism, Jehovah's Witness, New Age, Atheism and any other false religion. I also renounce unbelief, doubt, lies, fear, hatred and anger. I bind and cast out all related spirits.

22. Demons, I command you to come out of the mouth now and never come back, in Jesus' name. Go to the pit!

23. I cancel every negative word spoken in dark and secret places against me by the blood of Jesus.

24. Surely, there is no enchantment and divination against me.

25. I condemn the tongue of the enemy that is designed to undermine God's agenda for my life, in the name of Jesus.

26. Mighty God of Jacob, command deliverance for Your people.

27. Let liberty and wholeness be my portion in the land of the living.

28. I bind all ancestral and familiar spirits. I break their hold, superstitions and control over my life.

29. I take authority over demonic spirits assigned to enforce generational curses over my offspring.

30. I destroy the curse of premature death. I and all members of my family shall live till old age, even a hundred and twenty years plus.

31. I annihilate the curse of poverty and lack from my life.

32. I expose Satan's strange fire, and I quench it with the fire of God.

33. I come against all elements of danger, in the name of Jesus.

34. I terminate demonic assignments over my life and my family right now, in the name of Jesus.

35. Generational blessings shall be my portion from now on. I decree it to be so, in Jesus' name.

36. I renounce and reject every right or claim of any idol or demonic entity over my life, due to my father's and forefathers' worship of them. I have been redeemed by the blood of the Lamb, and no idol or demon has power over me.

37. I am loyal, royal, and immovable to the cause of the eternal order.

38. I am chosen to be a protector of my borders and destroyer of demonic migration.

39. Lord, I destroy generational curses on the lives of my parents, brothers, sisters, uncles, aunts, cousins, nieces and nephews. I set them free by the power and authority that I have in Jesus Christ.

## SCRIPTURAL REFERENCES

| | |
|---|---|
| Romans 8:2 | For the law of the Spirit of life in Christ Jesus has made me free from the law of sin and death. |
| Galatians 3:13 | Christ has redeemed us from the curse of the law, having become a curse for us. |
| Psalm 107:2 | Let the redeemed of the Lord say so, Whom He has redeemed from the hand of the enemy. |
| John 8:36 | Therefore if the Son makes you free, you shall be free indeed. |
| 1 John 3:8 | He who sins is of the devil, for the devil has sinned from the beginning. For this purpose the Son of God was manifested, that He might destroy the works of the devil. |
| Psalm 31:7 | I will be glad and rejoice in Your mercy, For You have considered my trouble; You have known my soul in adversities, And have not shut me up into the hand of the enemy; You have set my feet in a wide place. |
| Numbers 23:23 | "For there is no sorcery against Jacob, Nor any divination against Israel. |

# PRAYERS FOR BREAKING THE CYCLES OF SATANIC BONDAGE

***Job 22:28***
***Thou shalt also decree a thing, and it shall be established***
***unto thee: and the light shall shine upon thy ways.***

Father, in the name of Jesus, I stand upon Your Word. You said I shall decree a thing and it shall be established. You said whatever I permit here in the Earth realm and in my life shall be permitted in Heaven. I come boldly before the throne of grace to obtain mercy and find favor to help in my time of need. I appropriate the mercy of God on my own behalf and on the behalf of my family. I invoke the blood of Jesus right now against all satanic ploys, calculations, and against cycles of defeat and failure. In the name of Jesus and by the power of the atoning blood, I cancel all demonic predictions, calculations, manipulations, manifestations, and prophecies.

I thank You for seating me in Heavenly places and for blessing me with all spiritual blessings. In the name of Jesus, I come against ill will. I take my authority and I bind, blind, mute and deafen every foul spirit of Satan's kingdom, including principalities, powers of darkness in heavenly places, demonic spirits, fallen angels, hybrids and multi-dimensional spirits that have come against my house, family, health, prosperity, spiritual maturity, relationships, jobs, ministry, advertisements, websites, and all of the outreaches, projects, and operations that will expand the Kingdom of God. I cast those spirits to the pit, in Jesus' name. I loose in its place and set in motion the cycles of victory and success, in the name of Jesus. The devil's hold on me is totally broken. I interrupt every demonic agenda and assignment for my life. I command Satan's intentions for my life to die in the womb, and I command his purposes to fail, in the name of Jesus. I abort every satanic predication and demonic attack over my mind and my spirit, in the name of Jesus. I break the cycles of sin, depression, oppression, suppression, and obsession by the tokens of the blood of Jesus. I break all forms of bondage off my life. I break cycles of disfavor and ill will in my life and in my family, in the name of Jesus.

Your Word declares that You will not withhold any good thing from me because I walk uprightly. Your Word also says that there is no want to them that fear You. The young lions do lack, and suffer hunger, but they that seek the Lord shall not want any good thing. I break the cycles of financial stagnation by the power of the blood of Jesus. I place a perpetual injunction over all satanic harassment and aggravation. I break cycles of all satanic activity from my life and my family. I set into motion the anointing of the Holy Spirit in my life and in my family to release deliverance, salvation, restoration, protection and provision, in the name of Jesus.

I also call destructive fire down on all satanic organizations, occult covens, demonic corporations, businesses, governments, religions, Ponzi schemes, drug smuggling operations, human smuggling organizations, weapon smuggling operations, high places, financial support systems that support demonic agents, media, propaganda, and agendas on the Earth, in the Earth, in the heavenlies, and in the universe.

Father God, You have exalted my horn like the horn of the unicorn. You have anointed me with fresh oil. My eye also shall see my desire on mine enemies, and mine ears shall hear my desire of the wicked that rise up against me. Father, You are my light and my salvation, and I shall fear no man and no demonic spirit. The Lord is the strength of my life, and no one will frighten me. Any attempt of the wicked, even mine enemies, to attack me shall stumble and fall. Though a host should surround me, my heart shall not fear; though war should rise against me, in this will I be confident, because the Lord is for me and on my side. The forces of darkness that militated against my fathers will not succeed against me because I am a child of God. I am His beloved and ambassador, and I exercise my divine authority over them. Their assignments over my life and family have been terminated, in the name of Jesus.

I loose the power of God for divine advancement, progress, promotion, acceleration, and elevation in my life. I send forth the arrows of God's deliverance into my future for deliverance from every seen and unseen adversary. I loose the blood of Jesus against the eye of jealousy (outward) and envy (inward). I repel every satanic maneuver against me, in the name of Jesus.

I bind all forms of spells, curses, divination enchantments and satanic encroachments. I place an injunction over them, in the name of Jesus. I release the fire of God to burn to ashes every demonic foundation in my life, in Jesus' name. I loose the blood of Jesus against their operations. I overrule their agendas against me and overturn their conference tables, in the name of Jesus. I declare that I have world-overcoming faith residing in me, therefore, I have overcome the world, and the spiritual warfare that came through this world's systems, in the mighty name of Jesus. I declare that I am spiritually, physically, and financially stable, in Jesus' name.

I declare that the angels of the Living God have encamped round about me, and are delivering me right now. I will not dash my foot against a stone. I declare that God will satisfy me with long life, and He will show me His salvation. I declare that greater is He who is in me than He who is in the world. I declare that I rule in the midst of my enemies, and I have the upper hand in every situation in Jesus' name. Amen.

# Prayers to Bind the Spirit of Death and Suicide

### *Psalm 118:1-7*
### *I shall not die, but live, and declare the works of the Lord.*

1. Great and Mighty God, You are the Giver and Sustainer of my life.

2. I come against the spirit of death in my life. I command you, in the name of Jesus, to be bound and be cast to the bottomless pit.

3. I cover my spirit, my soul, my body with the blood of Jesus Christ as my protection.

4. I shall not die, but live and declare the works of the Lord. I shall live out my days, purpose, even a hundred and twenty years plus, according to the promise of God.

5. Death, you have no power over me, for I have been redeemed by the blood of Jesus Christ. I have been translated from the kingdom of darkness into the Kingdom of Light. I have been brought from death to life.

6. I destroy every branch and manifestation of death, and the demons that enforce them by the power of the Holy Spirit.

7. I destroy the forces behind untimely deaths, in the name of Jesus.

8. I loose myself from all satanic entanglements, in the name of Jesus.

9. Christ came to give me life and life in abundance. I claim that abundance right now, in Jesus' name.

10. Lord, You said You would satisfy me with long life, and fulfill the number of my days on Earth.

11. I bind the spirits of fear, depression, and suicide. I command the angels of God to arrest you and handcuff you by your hands and legs, and send you back to hell where you belong, in Jesus' name.

12. Father, I thank You for rescuing me from the jaws of death and saving me from the grave.

13. Father, because You protect and keep me as the apple of Your eyes, nothing can overcome me.

14. I humbly bow before Your holy throne in worship and adoration. Blessed be the Lord, because You have heard the voice of my prayers.

15. My heart trusts in You, O God, and I am helped. My heart greatly rejoices, and with new songs will I praise You. You are my God forever. My life is in Your hands.

## SCRIPTURAL REFERENCES

| | |
|---|---|
| Psalm 33:18 | Behold, the eye of the Lord is on those who fear Him, on those who hope in His mercy, to deliver their soul from death, and to keep them alive in famine. |
| Psalm 23:4 | Yea, though I walk through the valley of the shadow of death, I will fear no evil; for you are with me; Your rod and Your staff, they |

comfort me.

# PRAYERS AGAINST DEPRESSION

## *Nehemiah 8:10*
### *Do not sorrow, for the joy of the Lord is your strength.*

1. Dear God and Father of all mercies, I thank and bless Your holy name for the gift of prayer.
2. Dear soul, why are you disquieted within me? Hope in the Lord, and rejoice in His great mercies.
3. I will cry to God Most High, the God who performs all things for me.
4. Lord, bring my soul out of depression. Anoint my head with the oil of gladness, and clothe me with garments of praise.
5. Release the oil of gladness upon my life, removing the spirits of heaviness, depression, oppression, suicide, guilt, rejection and worthlessness, in Jesus' name.
6. I ask that You correct any chemical imbalance in my body due to the presence of evil spirits, replacing their presence with the presence of the Holy Spirit, restoring my peace, joy and righteousness in the Holy Spirit.
7. For this is the day that the Lord has made; I shall rejoice and be glad in it. Help me Lord, to drink out of the river of Your pleasures.
8. In the multitudes of my thoughts and confusion within me, Your comfort delights my soul.

9. Lord, let peace, like an ocean, engulf my soul. Let joy unspeakable and full of glory, joy like a river, fill my heart now, in Jesus' name.

10. I strongly rebuke the spirit of depression and command it to leave me alone right now, in Jesus' name. I paralyze the workings of the enemy in my soul. Amen.

## SCRIPTURAL REFERENCES

| | |
|---|---|
| John 14:27 | Peace I leave with you, My peace I give to you; not as the world gives do I give to you. Let not your heart be troubled, neither let it be afraid. |
| Isaiah 26:3 | You will keep him in perfect peace, Whose mind is stayed on You, Because he trusts in You. |
| Philippians 4:7 | And the peace of God, which surpasses all understanding, will guard your hearts and minds through Christ Jesus. |
| 2 Thessalonians 3:16 | Now may the Lord of peace Himself give you peace always in every way. The Lord be with you all. |
| Isaiah 26:12 | Lord, You will establish peace for us, For You have also done all our works [a]in us. |
| Isaiah 32:17 | The work of righteousness will be peace, And the effect of righteousness, quietness and assurance forever. |

| Isaiah 32:18 | My people will dwell in a peaceful habitation, In secure dwellings, and in quiet resting places. |
|---|---|

# PRAYERS FOR WORRY AND ANXIETY

***Matthew 6:25***
***Therefore I say to you, do not worry about your life, what you will eat or what you will drink; nor about your body, what you will put on. Is not life more than food and the body more than clothing?***

Having a consistent study and an effective prayer life are the solutions to anxiety and worry. The Word of God gives us hope, strengthens our faith, and allows us to hold on to our entire inheritance in Christ. When you are filled with the Word of God, you cannot be the victim of anxiety and worry. Mark 9:23 tells us that anything is possible for those who believe in the Word, while Matthew 17:20 tells us that with faith in the Word of God, we can move all mountains.

When you are filled with the Word of God in your inner man, you cannot be a victim of anxiety and worry. Prayers are also another antidote to anxiety and worry. A Christian praying is a powerful Christian. And a powerful Christian cannot be a victim of anxiety and worry. I have put together some powerful prayers to help you overcome the worry and fear in your life. I encourage you to participate with all your heart in these prayers. I see you living a carefree life, in the name of Jesus Christ.

1. The Holy Scriptures tell us to not worry about anything, but with prayers and thanksgiving, we are to present our requests to God. Lord, give me the strength not to be overwhelmed by a flood of worries and anguish. Father, help me to keep hope and believe in You; give me the grace to never lose faith in You, and give me the faith to know that You will overcome all fear and anxiety, in the name of Jesus.

2. Heavenly Father, You know the thoughts that flow through my heart. You know my fears and worries, even though many may think that I am always steadfast and high above my situation. Nevertheless, only You know that it consumes me quickly. Lord, I ask for Your help. My Father, send me help, in the name of Jesus.

3. The Bible says that the Spirit that God has given us does not make us timid, but gives us strength, love and self-discipline. Lord, I am hungry for this Spirit who will wash away my worries; I am thirsty for this Spirit who will give me power over all my fears and worries, in the name of Jesus.

4. Heavenly King of Glory, the Bible says that You did not give us the spirit of fear, but the Spirit of Your Son to cry out, "Abba, Father!" Lord, when the storms of life rage against me, when the painful roads ahead of me seem steep, and I can't help but breathe deeply, give me a heart of gratitude. You died on the cross for my sins. You gave Your life for the redemption of my soul out of the darkness. How much confidence and proof

do I need to believe You will help me? Lord, when they increase my anxiety and worry, You give me the grace to deal with all my problems, in the name of Jesus.

5. Even though I walk through the valley of the shadow of death, I am not afraid because You are with me. Your rod and Your reed comfort me. Lord, restore the rest of my soul to me by Your grace. Comfort me, in the name of Jesus. Isaiah 41:10 says that when worry was great within me, Your comfort brought me joy. Lord Jesus, You are the Prince of Peace. I ask You to make my house Your humble home and to give me peace in the arms of Jesus.

6. Lord Jesus, the Bible made it clear to me that You care very much for me and that I can express all my concerns to You, for it is You who are seated on the throne. Father, I leave all my worries to You. I transfer all of my worries to You; please don't let me be ashamed. You never made a promise that You didn't keep. The Bible lets me know that You raised Your Word above Your name. Lord, please keep all Your promises about me, in Jesus' name.

7. Jehovah God, I pray for the men and women whose souls are deeply troubled and eager to be comforted by Your Spirit. Please open their eyes to understanding, and show them how much You love them. Grant them the grace to cast all of their worries and anxieties on You. I pray that You give them joy in return, in Jesus' name.

8. Dear most Merciful and Heavenly Father, I'm afraid, I'm worried and I am anxious. I don't know what will happen to me, my neighbors, my country or even this world. I need You more than ever. I need You to hug and hold me. Remind me day-by-day, hour-by-hour, minute-by-minute and second-by-second that You are here. Love me. In the name of Jesus. Amen.

9. Heavenly Father, help me all my days. Teach me not to worry. Remind me not to worry. As it is written in Philippians, "Do not worry about anything, but in everything, by prayer and thanksgiving, proclaim your requests to God." I am now asking You to intervene because I need help. I need You. Thank You. Amen.

10. Dear God, I come before You and I place my fears and anxiety at Your feet. Please help me get rid of all doubts and fears when I feel overwhelmed. Remind me that You are a Mighty God. Remind me that I can trust You. I know I can't do it alone. I need You. In the incomparable name of Jesus, I pray. Amen.

11. This is the day the Lord has made, and I will rejoice and be glad in it. Thank You, Father, for the power of choice. Today, I choose to call upon the name of Jesus and the power of Your Word. My prayers are backed by the anointing of Christ to defeat the enemy's presence and the voices of fear, anxiety, and stress.

12. For You have not given me a spirit of fear, anxiety, or stress, but You have given me power, love, and a sound mind of Christ. As a new creation in Christ, old

things must pass away, bringing me into the new things of Christ.

13. Almighty God, I come before You now with my load of cares, and I lay them at Your feet.

14. It is written, cast your cares upon the Lord, for He cares for you. I know that You care for me, Lord.

15. I refuse to worry; rather, I choose to trust You. I refuse to fret. I refuse to panic in my present situation, for You, O Lord, are the strength of my life. Of whom shall I be afraid?

16. I repent for opening the door to the spirits of fear, anxiety, and stress in my family line, and anything I've done by sin or association. Wash me with the blood of Jesus Christ, and remove these spirits from my spirit, soul, body, members, memory, and mind. As Your offspring and joint heir, I take my authority over, rebuke, and break all powers of the enemy, and I loose myself from the spirits of fear, anxiety, and stress, in the name of Jesus. I cast them out of my spirit, soul, body, mind and members, and send them to the pit right now, in Jesus' Name.

17. I break and loose myself from all emotional attachments to fear, anxiety, stress, and anxiousness, casting these spirits from me to the pit, in Jesus' Name.

18. I decree that the peace of God will guide my heart and mind as I set my mind on Christ.

19. I receive Your promise of freedom from the enemy, and I welcome the Holy Spirit to replace the presence

of fear, stress, anxiety, and anxiousness. I call forth peace, joy, and righteousness, in Jesus' name.

20. You are my Shield, my Healer, my Great Provider, my Shepherd; I shall not want. For You make me to lie down in green pastures, and lead me besides the still, clean and crystal-clear waters.

21. You are my very present Help in times of trouble. For in the multitude of my thoughts within me, Your comforts delight my soul.

22. For if You, O Lord, be for me, You are more than the whole world who is against me.

23. For all things work together for the good of them that love the Lord and are called according to His purpose.

24. For I know even the present emergency, when all is said and done, will work for my ultimate good.

25. I strongly rebuke the spirit of fear, worry and anxiety in my life. I command you to leave right now, in the mighty name of Jesus. I bind and cast you all to the pit, in Jesus' name.

26. Lord, flood my soul with Your peace that surpasses all understanding now, and fill my heart with joy unspeakable. Amen.

27. I command the strongholds of worry, fear and anxiety in my life to crumble permanently, in Jesus' name.

28. I thank You, Lord, for the full assurance that You will never leave me nor forsake me.

29. I thank You, Jesus, for the price You paid on the cross. The power of Your blood and the Spirit of the Living

God has set me free. I give Jesus all glory for my freedom today. Amen.

# CONFESSION PRAYERS ON WORRY AND FEAR

I am the body of Christ, and Satan has no dominion over me. I overcome evil with good. I am of God, and have overcome the wicked one, for greater is He who is in me than he who is in the world. Though I walk through the valley of the shadow of death, I will fear no evil, for God is with me. His rod and His staff, His Word and His Spirit, they comfort me. No weapon formed against me prospers, and every tongue that rises against me in judgment, I condemn. If God be for me, who can be against me?

God did not spare His own Son, but delivered Him up for my sake. Through Him, He also freely gives me all things. No one can lay any charge on me. I am God's elect. God justifies me. No one can condemn me. It is Christ who died and is risen again, who is even at the right-hand side of God making intercession for me. This is my heritage because I am a servant of the Lord, and my righteousness is of God. I am delivered from the evils of this present world. The Lord preserves my life. He makes a way for me where there is no way. I am not hindered from entering any door that the Lord opens for me. The Lord delivers me out of the hand of the wicked. Light is radiated through me and gladness is in my heart. In my pathway, there is life and not death. I am a doer of the Word of God, and I am blessed in all my deeds. I am happy with the things that I do because I am a doer of the Word of God. I take the shield of faith and quench every fiery dart that the wicked one sends against me. I am submitted to God; therefore, the devil flees from me.

In the name of Jesus, I refuse to worry because my Heavenly Father takes care of me. I bind the spirit of fear from off my life. I am careful for nothing, but in everything by prayer and supplication with thanksgiving, I let my requests be made known unto God. The peace of God, which surpasses all understanding, keeps my heart and mind through Christ Jesus. I think on those things that are true, honest, just, pure, lovely, and are of good report. I am blessed with a great mind. My mind is renewed by God's Word. My imagination is powerful. Every thought that is not of God, I take captive of, in the name of Jesus. I fear no evil, for God is with me. If God be for me, who can be against me? I refuse to fear those things that frighten other people, in the name of Jesus. I will not be shaken by fear. I am not afraid of the terrors by night, nor the arrows that fly by day, nor the pestilence that stalks in darkness, nor the destruction and hidden death that surprises and lay waste at noonday. Thousands fall at my side and ten thousands at my right hand, but it shall not come near me. I shall be a spectator, witnessing the reward of the wicked, because I dwell and abide in the secret place of His presence.

I am never afraid. I do not know fear. I have the spirit of power. I have the spirit of love and a sound mind. I am far from oppression, and sickness does not come near me. Jesus said that He would never leave me nor forsake me, so I say boldly, the Lord is my Helper and I am not afraid of what man can do. Jesus is my Light and my Salvation; who shall I fear or dread? In the name of Jesus, I terminate any satanic point of contact in my domain. If a host encamps around me, my heart will not fear. Even in war, I will be confident because the Lord is my stronghold. No evil shall befall me, neither shall any plague come close to my dwelling, for the Lord has given His angels special charge over me. The angels of the Lord take charge over me in this land, and I will not dash my foot against any stone. I will not stumble.

Christ redeemed me from the curse of the law, therefore, I forbid any sickness or disease from coming upon me. Every disease, virus, or germ that touches my body dies instantly. In the name of Jesus, every organ and tissue of my body functions perfectly. My body lines up with the Word of God and functions the way God created it to function. I forbid any malfunction in my body, in the name of Jesus. I am an overcomer, and I have overcome the enemy by the blood of the Lamb and the words of my testimony. I am submitted to God, and the devil flees from me because I resist him, in the name of Jesus. Sicknesses and diseases flee from me. I am alive and very well, in the name of Jesus.

The Word of God is forever settled in Heaven; therefore, I will establish His Word in my life. Great is the peace of my children because they are taught of the Lord. They are protected, blessed, and wealthy. They are strong, healthy, anointed, and wholesome. They have nothing missing in their lives. They love God and keep His commandments. I am a loved person. My life is blameless under all circumstances. I endure everything without weakness. I never fail, and there nothing broken in my life. The lives of my children are ordered of the Lord. No man can ruin and overthrow God's purposes for my life, even as it is written, "To subvert a man in his cause, the Lord does not approve." And who is he who speaks and it comes to pass, when the Lord has not commanded it? God's purposes for my life are on course, in the name of Jesus.

I am growing in grace and in the knowledge of God. I am the redeemed of the Lord and whatsoever I say is so. I cannot be denied. I have what I say.

Heavenly Father, thank You for Your love, Your provision, and Your protection over my life, as well as the lives of my family members.

I praise and adore You because I know that I am not afraid. Your Word says I'm as brave as a lion. I'm a righteous man because of the death of Jesus on the cross of Calvary. I refuse to be afraid of any problem or circumstance because I do not have the spirit of fear, but the spirit of strength, love and common sense. I don't need to fear because my God and my Heavenly Father, the Creator of Heaven and Earth, are always by my side. You said that You are always with me to the ends of the Earth. You assured me by Your Word that I should not be afraid, because You are with me. I can't be intimidated because You are my God. You strengthen me and help me. You back me with a winning right hand. Everyone who is angry with me will be ashamed and dishonorable. Those who oppose me will be reduced to nothing and will disappear. I will look for them, but I will not find them. Those who are at war with me will be reduced to nothing, and will no longer exist. You, Lord, my God, hold my right hand, and You said that I shouldn't be afraid because You will help me. I refuse to worry because You said in Your Word that I should not worry about anything other than prayer with gratitude to announce my request to You. I leave all my worries to You, because You care about me. I refuse to carry more loads because I cast them over Your shoulder.

I am not afraid of any situation or circumstance, for You are my Protector and my Facilitator. You told me in Your Word that I should not be afraid because You redeemed me; You called me by my name. I'm all Yours. When I cross the waters, You will be with me, and when I pass through the rivers, the waters will not overwhelm me. When I go through the fire, I will not be burned and the flame will not hurt me. I will not be afraid. Even though I pass through the valley of the shadow of death, I will not fear any harm, for You are with me; Your rod and Your reed have comforted me. You are setting the table for me in the presence of my enemies.

Overcome all terrible situations and circumstances for You, O God, are my Refuge and my Strength. You are an eternally present Helper in difficult times. Even if the Earth is removed and the mountains are transferred to the middle of the sea, and its waters howl and rage, I will not be afraid. Even if the mountains tremble from their swelling, I will not be afraid. There is a river whose current will rejoice in the city of God. The holy place of the tabernacle of the Most High God is in the middle of it. She won't move. God will help you just in time.

So, you spirit of fear that encompasses my memory, my mind and my emotions, wherever you are with accompanying symptoms, illnesses or ailments, pack your bags and step out, in Jesus' name! You don't have the right to stay and work on my body or in my head, because Jesus defeated your master, the devil, on the Cavalier cross. I am currently seated with Jesus Christ well above principalities, power and authority. I command you, in the name of Jesus, to come out of my mind and body, in the name of Jesus.

Angels, servant spirits, go and carry out my confession, in the name of Jesus. Amen.

# CONFESSIONS FOR CONFIDENCE AND STRENGTH

God is terrible out of His holy places: the God of Israel is He that gives strength and power unto me. You are our strength and song we sing; You are our God and we praise You and we exalt Your wonderful name. You have guided us in Your strength to Your holy habitation. You are releasing a huge tidal wave of Your strength. I am increasing in the knowledge of God. I am strengthened with all might, according to His glorious power. My new strength is not like my old strength. God, restore to me the former glory and strengthen the latter glory, in the name of Jesus. I am delivered from the power of darkness, and I am translated into the Kingdom of His dear Son. I am strong in the Lord and in the power of His might. I put on the whole armor of God and I stand in the evil day. I am born of God and I have world overcoming faith residing on the inside of me. My faith is alive. I operate in the living faith anointing. Greater is He who is in me than he who is in the world. I can do all things through Christ who strengthens me.

I increase in wisdom and stature and in favor with God and man. The joy of the Lord is my strength. I trust not in the arm of the flesh, I put not confidence in a guide, I keep the doors of my mouth from the enemy. For the Lord is my confidence, and shall keep my foot from being taken. I rest in the Lord. I am saved. In quietness and in confidence is my strength. I am ready for, equal to, anything, through Him who infuses strength into me. God has infused me with strength. He has equipped, empowered, anointed me, crowned me with favor, put royal blood in my veins, called me to reign in life as a king. I dwell in a peaceable habitation, and in sure dwellings, and in quiet resting-places, which is the presence of God. The Lord is the strength of my life, whom shall I be afraid? The peace of God, the Shalom of God, the wholeness of God, which surpasses all understanding, keeps my mind and my heart through Christ Jesus. I rejoice in the salvation of the Lord, and in the name of my God, I set up our banners. The Lord fulfills all my petitions. The Lord is a shield for me. He is my glory and the lifter of my head. The Lord saves His anointed. The Lord hears me from His holy Heaven with the saving strength of His right hand. Some trust in chariots and some in horses, but I remember the name of the Lord, my God. They are brought down and fallen, but I am elevated and strong.

I declare that I am anointed for this. I am built for this. I can handle it. I know God is on the throne, fighting my battles, and if God be for me who dare be against me? I am full of can-do power, for the end has already been set; the greater the intensity, the closer I am to my victory.

My God supplies all my needs according to His riches in glory by Christ Jesus. I have no need, in the name of Jesus. All my needs are met. I speak the truth of the Word of God, and in my pathway are not lies. I walk in love and I grow up in the Lord. I please Christ in all things. No man shall take me out of His hands. Now, I allow the peace of God to rule in my heart and I refuse to fret or to be anxious and worry about anything. I cast all my burdens and cares upon God because He cares for me. Care, fear, worry and anxiety go now, in the name of Jesus. The Lord keeps me now in perfect peace because my mind is stayed on Him and His Word. The Word of God will not slip from me nor depart from my eyes. I will do everything I need to do to keep the Word of God in my heart. For I esteem His Word more than my necessary food.

The Word of God rules my life. My emotions and circumstances do not rule me. I refuse to be aggravated. I am ruled by His Word. The Word is life to me. It is health, healing, and medicine to all my flesh. I keep my heart with all diligence. I do not sin against God because I keep the Word of God in my heart. I have great peace because I love the Word of God, and nothing offends me. I have the world overcoming faith residing on the inside of me.

God is with me now. God is alive in me. He is on my side, so who can be against me? He did not spare His only Son, but delivered Him for me. Who can lay any charge on me? God is my Justifier. Who can condemn me? He has given me all things that pertain to life and Godliness because I am filled with the knowledge of His love. I am a partaker of His divine nature. God's favor is for life. Weeping may endure for a period, but my joy comes in the morning. I pass through the

Valley of Baca (weeping), but I have made it a blessing. I go from strength to strength. I am strong in the Lord and the power of His might. I put on the whole armor of God and I am able to stand in the evil day. I am a believer; therefore, signs and wonders do follow me.

I am anointed. Jesus gave me the authority to use His name. Satan, I bind you, in the name of Jesus. I place an injunction over all your demons. I loose the blood of Jesus against you. I draw the blood-stained banner against you. I appeal to the blood of Jesus, which is my stronghold. I restrain every power of darkness, in the name of Jesus. In the name of Jesus Christ, I bind all principalities and powers and refuse them access into my life. I bind every enforcer of curses in my life and family, in the name of Jesus. I bind the rulers of darkness and spiritual wickedness in high places and render them powerless and harmless against me, in the name of Jesus. I loose angels now to do the bidding of God; hearken to His Word, go forth and bring my harvest now. Go now and bring forth my promotion. I will not be under any financial crisis. The financial seeds that I have sown forces the future to whimper at my feet like a puppy begging for instruction. I will experience the miracle of debt cancellation. All my bills are paid now. All my debts are canceled, in the name of Jesus. I superimpose the prophetic purposes of God over every agenda of the enemy. I cancel every satanic prediction, calculation, counsel and purpose by the speaking of the blood of Jesus. I declare that every positive word spoken concerning my life will come to pass. I activate every prophetic purpose of God for my life.

I position myself for wealth transfer. I cannot be poor because Jesus took my poverty with Him on the cross. Wealth comes to me now, in the name of Jesus. Now, angels go, and bring to pass all the words that I have spoken. I have a promotion. I am successful. The favor of God is upon me now. Whatever I do proposers. I do not cast away my confidence, which has great recompense of reward. I do the will of God, and I receive the promise. All the horns of the wicked the Lord cuts off, but my horns are exalted. I am anointed with fresh oil. God gives power to me, and He increases my strength. Even the youth faint and become weary, and the young men utterly fall, but because I wait upon the Lord, He renews my strength. I mount up with wings as eagles; I run, and I am not weary, and I walk, and do not faint. My God had commanded my strength: strengthen, O God, that which You have done for us. I am the redeemed of the Lord and whatsoever I say is so. I cannot be denied. I have what I say. Amen.

# CONFESSION OF GREATNESS

I am a fruitful bough, even a fruitful bough by a well; my branches run over the wall. My branches run over every wall of satanic and demonic resistances, opposition, restrictions and limitations, wants, lack and setbacks. I shall bounce back, in Jesus' name. My life abides in His strength and my arms were made strong by the hands of the Almighty God of Jacob. I am becoming great now. God prospers me on every side.

The Almighty God helps me and blesses me with the blessings of Heaven above and the blessings deep that lies beneath, according to the Word of God. I delight myself in the Lord, and He grants me the desires of my heart because my desires line up with the Word of God. I am out of debt now. I do not have bad credit. My credit score is perfect. I will not be refused at any time or anywhere for anything that I need. As soon as people see me, they will help me; this includes my enemies.

I love His Word, and therefore, I have great peace and nothing offends me. I cannot be offended. I live above offense. I have given of my abundance, and the blessings of God are given unto me in good measure, pressed down, shaken together, and running over, men are giving unto my bosom. I am truly blessed of the Lord. I tithe and giving offerings. Therefore, the windows of Heaven are open to me, and I have abundance. I live in pleasure. I have more in store to do in the will of God. The devourer cannot destroy the works of my hands. I am not cursed. I am blessed. The blessings of the Lord upon my life affect those with whom I come in contact. For with what measure I give, it is measured unto me. God supplies me with seed for my sowing.

I reap the harvest. My harvest is coming to me from the east to the west, and from the north to the south. I am spreading northward, southward, eastward, and westward. I am honorable. I am well-favored. I am very precious in God's eyes. God increases my greatness and comforts me on every side. The blessings of Abraham are mine. The blessings of favor, wealth, wisdom, prosperity, long life, and righteousness are mine. I sow bountifully, therefore, I reap bountifully. I give cheerfully; therefore, God has allowed all grace to abound towards me. I have all sufficiency in all things and do abound to good works. I am a good steward of what God has given me. I have no lack, for God is my Shepherd and I shall not want. I shall not want in wealth, health, or power. I do not want because Jesus was made poor so that I may become rich. He came so that I may have life and have it more abundantly. I have received the abundance of grace, and righteousness does reign in my life by Christ Jesus. I am in right-standing with God.
I am the redeemed of the Lord, and whatsoever I say is so. I cannot be denied. I have what I say.

# Prayers of Sweet Sleep

## Psalm 4:8
*I will both lie down in peace, and sleep; For You alone, O Lord, make me dwell in safety.*

1. Father God, it is bedtime. I thank You for helping me throughout today.
2. I curse every corruptible seed that was implanted in me, and I command them to wither and die. I loose myself from every spirit associated with those seeds, in Jesus' name.
3. Father God, allow Your righteous seeds to grow and bear fruit for Your glory.
4. I now commit my spirit, my soul and my body into Your hands.
5. Send Your angels to come and guard this house, and watch over me while I sleep.
6. Lord, prohibit demonic interference in my dreams; stop all demonic visitations, in the mighty name of Jesus.
7. I bind all forces that cause nightmares to come near me or interfere with my dreams.
8. Lord, mortify and fortify my spirit against any evil manipulations in dreams.
9. I apply the blood of Jesus over my house, upon the roof, walls and floors, and upon all of my family

members, possessions, my car, my workplace, as well as my spirit, soul, body and dreams.

10. I bind up every spirit of terror, fear, nightmares, or torment. I bind every mind-binding, evil, foul, lying and unclean spirit that may try to come and torment me in any way by the blood of the Lamb.

11. I reject and refuse to eat any food or drink anything offered to me in dreams.

12. I muzzle the voice of the stranger. Satan, you and every evil spirit in your kingdom that is in or around this property, I bind you and drive you out, in the name of Jesus.

13. I reject and refuse to engage myself in immoral or sexual relationships with any being in my dream, in the mighty name of Jesus.

14. Any astral projection or soul traveling spirits that could be in or around this property, I give you an eviction notice. Your lease has been terminated, in the name of Jesus. Find your exit and go now, in Jesus' name!

15. Lord, though spiritual battles may rage around me, You will deliver me and protect me. Give me assurance that You will never leave me nor forsake me. May the peace of God reign in my life, the love of God surrounds me, the Spirit of God empowers me, and the joy of God upholds me.

16. Let Your glory shine and encompass me while I sleep.

17. Father God, send Your warring angels to watch over me and to hold back the forces of Satan and his Kingdom while I sleep.

18. Send Your ministering angels to come and minister to me as I sleep.

19. Holy Spirit, come and flow through me, giving me dreams, visions, health, supernatural rest, and let me wake up refreshed.

20. I ask for divine and God-inspired dreams, visions and revelations to fill my soul.

21. Lord, open my spiritual eyes, so that I can see clearly and vividly in dreams, and understand messages and warnings from Your throne. Lord, I thank You for dream interpretations, in the name of Jesus.

22. I pray for my loved ones, both far and near, that You would grant them with peaceful and restful sleep.

23. I pray for Your help of protection around them. I sprinkle the blood of Jesus Christ over their lives.

24. You are my Shield and my Fortress. I find security and everything I need in You.

25. May I sleep under the powerful protection of Your name tonight and every night.

Thank You Father, for this time of prayer. Good night. I love You.

# HOLY SPIRIT

***Romans 8:26***
***Likewise the Spirit also helps in our weaknesses. For we do not know what we should pray for as we ought, but the Spirit Himself makes intercession for us with groanings which cannot be uttered.***

1. Blessed Holy Spirit, help my weaknesses concerning prayer "for I know not what I should pray for as I ought."
2. Come, Holy Spirit, and give me the right thoughts and right words as I pray, O dear Friend and Teacher.
3. As the fire fell down on Elijah's sacrifice and licked up even the water that was in the trenches, so let the consuming fire of the Holy Spirit engulf my whole being, to burn off all impurities, lethargy, weaknesses and lukewarmness, purifying me in spirit, soul and body.
4. Holy Spirit, help me to give God befitting praise and worship. Come upon me like a fresh and invigorating wind, and fill me up to overflow with fresh anointing.
5. Help me to love Christ intensely, to love my fellow men sincerely, and to love the name of Jesus above everything.
6. Holy Spirit, come upon me. Saturate, sweeten, and perfume every fiber of my being with Your holy fragrance.

7. Help me to never to grieve nor vex You in any way. Help me never to show disrespect or quench You, O my dear Friend and Companion.

8. Spirit of the Living God, continue to travail in me and through me with groaning that cannot be uttered.

9. Eternal Spirit of the Most High God, draw and lead me by the hand beyond the veil and into the Holy of Holies. Draw me into Your very presence, God Almighty.

10. Holy Spirit, produce Your fruits of love, joy, peace, long-suffering, kindness, goodness, faithfulness, gentleness, and self-control in me.

11. Impart and activate Your spiritual gifts in me, even during the night.

12. Give me great insight into Your divine mysteries and blessed earthly treasures. Give me acute spiritual perception and discretion.

13. Sweet Spirit of the Living God, rekindle in me a burning desire, a fresh vision, an overwhelming zeal, and an intense passion for the things of God.

# Prayers to Increase My Sensitivity to the Holy Spirit

***Romans 8:14***
***For as many as are led by the Spirit of God, these are sons of God.***

1. Lord, my God, bless me with the grace of being led perpetually by Your Holy Spirit so that I may manifest the reality of being Your child forever.
2. Holy Spirit, stir me up for service to the Living God, in Jesus' name.
3. My Father and my God, cast me not away from Your presence and take not Your Holy Spirit from me.
4. Grant me, O Lord, a contrite and humble spirit so that Your Spirit will dwell with me and revive me.
5. Lord, let me never vex Your Holy Spirit.
6. Let a fresh anointing of Your Holy Spirit descend upon me today, and remain in me, in Jesus' name.
7. Lord, seal me with the Holy Spirit of promise.
8. Teach me to rely on the power of Your Spirit to accomplish all things.
9. Lord, pull out my spiritual antenna so that I may receive clear signs and directions from the Holy Spirit.
10. Grant me the peace of God that brings the presence of the Holy Spirit to make my life powerful and progressive forever. In Jesus' name. Amen.

# FRUIT OF THE HOLY SPIRIT

*Galatians 5:22*
*But the fruit of the Spirit is love, joy, peace, longsuffering, kindness, goodness, faithfulness, gentleness, self-control.*

Heavenly Father, I come to You now to thank and adore You for the marvelous gift of Your Spirit and Your presence that dwells within me.

1. Holy Spirit, produce the wonderful fruit of Love in my heart that I may love all men from a sincere heart.
2. Holy Spirit, fill my heart with joy unspeakable and fill it with glory. Let the joy of the Lord be continually my strength.
3. Let **peace**, like a river, flood my soul. This is the peace of God that surpasses all understanding.
4. Holy Spirit, produce abundant **patience**, **long-suffering** and endurance in me.
5. Give me a tender and **kind** heart. Help me to be kind to all, both kind in words and in deed in everything I do.
6. Give me the grace to be **good** at all times. Help me to be good, even to my enemies.
7. Help me to be **faithful** in everything I do, for it is written, "The faithful soul shall abound with many blessings."

8. Lord, clothe me with the spirit of humility and **gentleness**. Let not harsh words ever come out of my mouth.

9. Lord, impart unto me the fruit of **self-control**. Give me the supernatural ability to control myself when tempted or provoked. Instill in me self-discipline, diligence, and self-restraint.

Thank You, Lord, for producing these fruits in my life. I pray that You will maximize the growth and maturity of these fruits to the honor and glory of Your name. Amen. And it is so!

# GIFTS OF THE HOLY SPIRIT

*1 Corinthians 14:1*
*Pursue love, and desire spiritual gifts, but especially that*
*You may prophesy.*

Father God, I thank You for the gift of Your Spirit who dwells, lives and moves in me.

Activate the nine gifts of the Holy Spirit in my life and ministry. Give me wisdom and discretion in maximizing the operation of these gifts for the edifying, equipping and establishing of the saints of God in faith and righteousness.

1. Holy Spirit, activate the gift of the **word of wisdom** in me, so as to be able to counsel the saints of God with the right words in their needful hour, for the counsel of God endures forever.
2. Impart to me the gift of the **word of knowledge**. Open my spiritual eyes, discernment, keenness, and ears so that I may see and hear. Give me an active spiritual perception.
3. Impart unto me the gift of **faith**, so that I can walk and minister in the realm of supernatural faith and move all mountains.
4. Holy Spirit, impart to me the gift of **healing**, so that all kinds of sicknesses and diseases will be healed through the power of prayer.

5. Holy Spirit, I ask for the gift of **miracles**. Perform signs, wonders and miracles in the lives of those that I minister to and pray for.

6. Holy Spirit, impart unto me the gift of **prophecy**, the supernatural ability to edify, encourage, and comfort Your people through prophetic utterances.

7. Holy Spirit, give me the gift of **discerning of spirits**. Lord, in these last days where there are all kinds of spirits and manifestations, I need this gift to be able to discern accurately, and test all spirits to make sure they are of You.

8. Holy Spirit, give me the gift of **divers kinds of tongues**. I need these supernatural utterances for effective intercession and spiritual warfare, for I know not how to pray as I ought.

9. Holy Spirit, give me the gift of the **interpretation of tongues**. Give me the supernatural ability to understand and interpret all divine utterances.

Thank You, Holy Spirit, for imparting these gifts and manifesting them through me. To God alone be all the glory for the souls that shall be blessed by these gifts. Amen.

# THE SINNER'S PRAYERS

*Isaiah 1:18*
*"Come now, and let us reason together," says the Lord, "Though your sins are like scarlet, They shall be as white as snow; Though they are red like crimson, They shall be as wool."*

1. Heavenly Father, I come to You in the name of Jesus. Your Word says, "Him that cometh to me I will in no wise cast out" (John 6:37).
2. It is written in Your Word, "If I confess with my mouth that Lord Jesus, and shall believe in my heart that God hath raised Him from the dead, I shall be saved. For whosoever shall call upon the name of the Lord shall be saved" (Romans 10:9-13).
3. I believe in my heart that Jesus Christ is the Son of God, and I confess with my mouth the Lord Jesus as my Savior and Deliverer.
4. Lord Jesus, I come to You by faith, just as I am. I am a sinner. Have mercy on me. I apologize and I'm sorry for my sins. I ask for Your forgiveness and pardon.
5. Lord Jesus, wash my spirit, my soul, and body with Your blood which was shed on the cross of Calvary for me.
6. Lord Jesus, I open the door of my heart to You right now by faith, and I invite You to come into my heart

to be my Lord and Savior from now and throughout eternity.

7.  Write my name in Your Book of Life, and give me the power to become a child of God, according to John 1:12, which reads, "But as many as received Him, to them He gave the power to become children of God, to those who believe in His name."

8.  Devil, listen, I hereby renounce and reject you. I command you and your cohorts to get out of my life, my borders, and my future, in Jesus' name.

9.  I hereby break and revoke every vow, promise, covenant, oath, tie, relationship, allegiance made or pledge to you directly or indirectly, knowingly or unknowingly, in the name of the Lord Jesus.

10. My Heavenly Father, I thank You, for hearing my prayers and saving my soul. I am now a born-again child of God, and I vow to follow and serve You for the rest of my life. Amen.

## SCRIPTURAL REFERENCES

| | |
|---|---|
| Matthew 11:28 | Come to Me, all you who labor and are heavy laden, and I will give you rest. |
| Proverbs 28:13 | He who covers his sins will not prosper, But whoever confesses and forsakes them will have mercy. |
| Isaiah 1:18 | "Come now, and let us reason together," Says the Lord, "Though your sins are like scarlet, They shall be as white as snow; Though they are red like crimson, They shall |

| | |
|---|---|
| | be as wool. |
| Isaiah 55:7 | Let the wicked forsake his way, And the unrighteous man his thoughts; Let him return to the Lord, And He will have mercy on him; And to our God, For He will abundantly pardon. |
| John 3:16 | For God so loved the world that He gave His only begotten Son, that whoever believes in Him should not perish but have everlasting life. |
| John 1:12 | But as many as received Him, to them He gave the right to become children of God, to those who believe in His name. |
| Romans 10:10 | For with the heart one believes unto righteousness, and with the mouth confession is made unto salvation. |
| Romans 10:13 | For "whoever calls on the name of the Lord shall be saved." |

# DANIEL'S PRAYER AND SUPPLICATION FOR JERUSALEM

*Daniel 9:3-9:23*
*Then I set my face toward the Lord God to make request by prayer and supplications, with fasting, sackcloth, and ashes.*

And I prayed to the Lord my God, and made confession, and said, "O Lord, great and awesome God, who keeps His covenant and mercy with those who love Him, and with those who keep His commandments, we have sinned and committed iniquity, we have done wickedly and rebelled, even by departing from Your precepts and Your judgments. Neither have we heeded Your servants the prophets, who spoke in Your name to our kings and our princes, to our fathers and all the people of the land. O Lord, righteousness belongs to You, but to us shame of face, as it is this day—to the men of Judah, to the inhabitants of Jerusalem and all Israel, those near and those far off in all the countries to which You have driven them, because of the unfaithfulness which they have committed against You. "O Lord, to us belongs shame of face, to our kings, our princes, and our fathers, because we have sinned against You. To the Lord our God belong mercy and forgiveness, though we have rebelled against Him. We have not obeyed the voice of the Lord our God, to walk in His laws, which He set before us by His servants the prophets. Yes, all Israel has transgressed Your law, and has departed so as not to obey Your voice; therefore the curse and the oath written in the Law of Moses the servant of God have been poured out on us, because we have sinned against Him. And He has confirmed His words, which He spoke against us and against our judges who judged us, by bringing upon us a great disaster; for under the whole heaven such has never been done as what has been done to Jerusalem. "As it is written in the Law of Moses, all this disaster has come upon us; yet we have not made our prayer before the Lord our God, that we might turn from our iniquities and understand Your truth. Therefore the Lord has kept the disaster in mind, and brought it upon us; for the Lord our God is righteous in all the works which He does, though we have not obeyed His voice. And now, O Lord our God, who brought Your people out of the land of Egypt with a mighty hand, and made Yourself a name, as it is this day— we have sinned, we have done wickedly! "O Lord, according to all Your righteousness, I pray, let Your anger and Your fury be turned away from Your city Jerusalem, Your holy mountain; because for our sins, and for the iniquities of our fathers, Jerusalem and Your people are a reproach to all those around us. Now therefore, our God, hear the prayer of Your servant, and his supplications, and for the Lord's sake cause Your face to shine on Your sanctuary, which is desolate. O my God, incline Your ear and hear; open Your eyes and see our desolations, and the city which is called by Your name; for we do not present our supplications before You because of our righteous deeds, but because of Your great mercies. O Lord, hear! O Lord, forgive! O Lord, listen and act! Do not delay for Your own sake, my God, for Your city and Your people are called by Your name." Now while I was speaking, praying, and confessing my sin and the sin of my people Israel, and presenting my supplication before the Lord my God for the holy mountain of my God, yes, while I was speaking in prayer, the man Gabriel, whom I had seen in the vision at the beginning, being caused to fly swiftly, reached me about the time of the evening offering. And he informed me, and talked with me, and said, "O Daniel, I have now come forth to give you skill to understand. At the beginning of your supplications the command went out, and I have come to tell you, for you are greatly beloved; therefore, consider the matter, and understand the vision."

# NEHEMIAH'S PRAYER WHILE IN CAPTIVITY

## *Nehemiah 1:3-11*

And they said to me, "The survivors who are left from the captivity in the province are there in great distress and reproach. The wall of Jerusalem is also broken down, and its gates are burned with fire." So it was, when I heard these words, that I sat down and wept, and mourned for many days; I was fasting and praying before the God of heaven. And I said: "I pray, Lord God of heaven, O great and awesome God, You who keep Your covenant and mercy with those who love You and observe Your commandments, please let Your ear be attentive and Your eyes open, that You may hear the prayer of Your servant which I pray before You now, day and night, for the children of Israel Your servants, and confess the sins of the children of Israel which we have sinned against You. Both my father's house and I have sinned. We have acted very corruptly against You, and have not kept the commandments, the statutes, nor the ordinances which You commanded Your servant Moses. Remember, I pray, the word that You commanded Your servant Moses, saying, 'If you are unfaithful, I will scatter you among the nations; but if you return to Me, and keep My commandments and do them, though some of you were cast out to the farthest part of the heavens, yet I will gather them from there, and bring them to the place which I have chosen as a dwelling for My name.' Now these are Your servants and Your people, whom You have redeemed by Your great power, and by Your strong hand. O Lord, I pray, please let Your ear be attentive to the prayer of Your servant, and to the prayer of Your servants who desire to fear Your name; and let Your servant prosper this day, I pray, and grant him mercy in the sight of this man." For I was the king's cupbearer.

# Israel's National Prayer of Repentance

*Nehemiah 9:5-38*
*Stand up and bless the Lord your God Forever and ever!*

Blessed be Your glorious name, Which is exalted above all blessing and praise! You alone are the Lord; You have made heaven, The heaven of heavens, with all their host, The earth and everything on it, The seas and all that is in them, And You preserve them all. The host of heaven worships You. "You are the Lord God, Who chose Abram, And brought him out of Ur of the Chaldeans, And gave him the name Abraham; You found his heart faithful before You, And made a covenant with him To give the land of the Canaanites, The Hittites, the Amorites, The Perizzites, the Jebusites, And the Girgashites— To give it to his descendants. You have performed Your words, for You are righteous. "You saw the affliction of our fathers in Egypt, And heard their cry by the Red Sea. You showed signs and wonders against Pharaoh, Against all his servants, And against all the people of his land. For You knew that they acted proudly against them. So You made a name for Yourself, as it is this day. And You divided the sea before them, So that they went through the midst of the sea on the dry land; And their persecutors You threw into the deep, As a stone into the mighty waters. Moreover You led them by day with a cloudy pillar, And by night with a pillar of fire, To give them light on the road Which they should travel. "You came down also on Mount Sinai, And spoke with them from heaven, And gave them just ordinances and true laws, Good statutes and commandments. You made known to them Your holy Sabbath, And commanded them precepts, statutes and laws, By the hand of Moses Your servant. You gave them bread from heaven for their hunger, And brought them water out of the rock for their thirst, And told them to go in to possess the land Which You had sworn to give them.

But they and our fathers acted proudly, hardened their necks, And did not heed Your commandments. They refused to obey, And they were not mindful of Your wonders That You did among them. But they hardened their necks, And in their rebellion They appointed a leader To return to their bondage. But You are God, Ready to pardon, Gracious and merciful, Slow to anger, Abundant in kindness, And did not forsake them. Even when they made a molded calf for themselves, And said, 'This is your god That brought you up out of Egypt,' And worked great provocations, yet in Your manifold mercies You did not forsake them in the wilderness. The pillar of the cloud did not depart from them by day, To lead them on the road; Nor the pillar of fire by night, To show them light, And the way they should go. You also gave Your good Spirit to instruct them, And did not withhold Your manna from their mouth, And gave them water for their thirst. Forty years You sustained them in the wilderness; They lacked nothing; Their clothes did not wear out And their feet did not swell. "Moreover You gave them kingdoms and nations, And divided them into districts. So they took possession of the land of Sihon, The land of the king of Heshbon, And the land of Og king of Bashan. You also multiplied their children as the stars of heaven, And brought them into the land Which You had told their fathers To go in and possess. So the people went in And possessed the land; You subdued before them the inhabitants of the land, The Canaanites, And gave them into their hands, With their kings And the people of the land, That they might do with them as they wished. And they took strong cities and a rich land, And possessed houses full of all goods, Cisterns already dug, vineyards, olive groves, And fruit trees in abundance. So they ate and were filled and grew fat, And delighted themselves in Your great goodness. "Nevertheless they were disobedient And rebelled against You, Cast Your law behind their backs And killed Your prophets, who testified against them To turn them to Yourself; And they worked great provocations. Therefore You delivered them into the hand of their enemies, Who oppressed them; And in the time of their trouble, When they cried to You, You heard from heaven; And according to Your abundant mercies You gave them deliverers who saved them From the hand of their enemies. "But after they had rest, They again did evil before You. Therefore You left them in the hand of their enemies, So that they had dominion over them; Yet when they returned and cried out to You, You heard from ; And many times You delivered them according to Your mercies, And testified against them, That You might bring them back to Your law.

Yet they acted proudly, And did not heed Your commandments, But sinned against Your judgments, 'Which if a man does, he shall live by them.' And they shrugged their shoulders, Stiffened their necks, And would not hear. Yet for many years You had patience with them, And testified against them by Your Spirit in Your prophets. Yet they would not listen; Therefore, You gave them into the hand of the peoples of the lands. Nevertheless, in Your great mercy You did not utterly consume them nor forsake them; For You are God, gracious and merciful. "Now therefore, our God, The great, the mighty, and awesome God, Who keeps covenant and mercy: Do not let all the trouble seem small before You That has come upon us, Our kings and our princes, Our priests and our prophets, Our fathers and on all Your people, From the days of the kings of Assyria until this day. However You are just in all that has befallen us; For You have dealt faithfully, But we have done wickedly. Neither our kings nor our princes, Our priests nor our fathers, Have kept Your law, Nor heeded Your commandments and Your testimonies, With which You testified against them. For they have not served You in their kingdom, Or in the many good things that You gave them, Or in the large and rich land which You set before them; Nor did they turn from their wicked works. "Here we are, servants today! And the land that You gave to our fathers, To eat its fruit and its bounty, Here we are, servants in it! And it yields much increase to the kings You have set over us, Because of our sins; Also they have dominion over our bodies and our cattle At their pleasure; And we are in great distress. "And because of all this, we

242

make a sure covenant and write it; Our leaders, our Levites, and our priests seal it."

# JACOB'S PRAYER BEFORE MEETING ESAU

*Genesis 32:9-12*
*Then Jacob said, "O God of my father Abraham and God of my father Isaac, the Lord who said to me, 'Return to your country and to your family, and I will deal well with you':*

I am not worthy of the least of all the mercies and of all the truth which You have shown Your servant; for I crossed over this Jordan with my staff, and now I have become two companies. Deliver me, I pray, from the hand of my brother, from the hand of Esau; for I fear him, lest he come and attack me and the mother with the children. For You said, 'I will surely treat you well, and make your descendants as the sand of the sea, which cannot be numbered for multitude.'

This prayer by Jacob was heard and answered by God. It turns the murderous hatred in the heart of Esau to brotherly hugs and kisses.

Genesis 33:4: But Esau ran to meet him, and embraced him, and fell on his neck and kissed him, and they wept.

# MOSES'S INTERCESSION FOR ISRAEL

*Numbers 14:11-20*
*Then the Lord said to Moses: "How long will these people reject Me? And how long will they not believe Me, with all the signs which I have performed among them?*

I will strike them with the pestilence and disinherit them, and I will make of you a nation greater and mightier than they." And Moses said to the Lord: "Then the Egyptians will hear it, for by Your might You brought these people up from among them, and they will tell it to the inhabitants of this land. They have heard that You, Lord, are among these people; that You, Lord, are seen face to face and Your cloud stands above them, and You go before them in a pillar of cloud by day and in a pillar of fire by night. Now if You kill these people as one man, then the nations which have heard of Your fame will speak, saying, 'Because the Lord was not able to bring this people to the land which He swore to give them, therefore He killed them in the wilderness.' And now, I pray, let the power of my Lord be great, just as You have spoken, saying, 'The Lord is longsuffering and abundant in mercy, forgiving iniquity and transgression; but He by no means clears the guilty, visiting the iniquity of the fathers on the children to the third and fourth generation.' Pardon the iniquity of this people, I pray, according to the greatness of Your mercy, just as You have forgiven this people, from Egypt even until now." Then the Lord said: "I have pardoned, according to your word."

# Joshua's Prayer after the Defeat at Ai

*Joshua 7:5-13*
*And the men of Ai struck down about thirty-six men, for they chased them from before the gate as far as Shebarim, and struck them down on the descent; therefore the hearts of the people melted and became like water.*

Then Joshua tore his clothes, and fell to the earth on his face before the ark of the Lord until evening, he and the elders of Israel; and they put dust on their heads. And Joshua said, "Alas, Lord God, why have You brought this people over the Jordan at all—to deliver us into the hand of the Amorites, to destroy us? Oh, that we had been content, and dwelt on the other side of the Jordan! O Lord, what shall I say when Israel turns its back before its enemies? For the Canaanites and all the inhabitants of the land will hear it, and surround us, and cut off our name from the earth. Then what will You do for Your great name?" So the Lord said to Joshua: "Get up! Why do you lie thus on your face? Israel has sinned, and they have also transgressed My covenant which I commanded them. For they have even taken some of the accursed things, and have both stolen and deceived; and they have also put it among their own stuff. Therefore the children of Israel could not stand before their enemies, but turned their backs before their enemies, because they have become doomed to destruction. Neither will I be with you anymore, unless you destroy the accursed from among you. Get up, sanctify the people, and say, 'Sanctify yourselves for tomorrow, because thus says the Lord God of Israel: "There is an accursed thing in your midst, O Israel; you cannot stand before your enemies until you take away the accursed thing from among you."

# KING HEZEKIAH'S PRAYER

*Isaiah 37:14-36*
*And Hezekiah received the letter from the hand of the*
*messengers, and read it; and Hezekiah went up to the*
*house of the Lord, and spread it before the Lord.*

Then Hezekiah prayed to the Lord, saying: "O Lord of hosts, God of Israel, the One who dwells between the cherubim, You are God, You alone, of all the kingdoms of the earth. You have made heaven and earth. Incline Your ear, O Lord, and hear; open Your eyes, O Lord, and see; and hear all the words of Sennacherib, which he has sent to reproach the living God. Truly, Lord, the kings of Assyria have laid waste all the nations and their lands, and have cast their gods into the fire; for they were not gods, but the work of men's hands— wood and stone. Therefore, they destroyed them. Now therefore, O Lord our God, save us from his hand, that all the kingdoms of the earth may know that You are the Lord, You alone." Then Isaiah the son of Amoz sent to Hezekiah, saying, "Thus says the Lord God of Israel, 'Because you have prayed to Me against Sennacherib king of Assyria, this is the word which the Lord has spoken concerning him: "The virgin, the daughter of Zion, Has despised you, laughed you to scorn; The daughter of Jerusalem Has shaken her head behind your back! "Whom have you reproached and blasphemed? Against whom have you raised your voice, And lifted up your eyes on high? Against the Holy One of Israel. By your servants you have reproached the Lord, And said, 'By the multitude of my chariots I have come up to the height of the mountains, To the limits of Lebanon; I will cut down its tall cedars And its choice cypress trees; I will enter its farthest height, To its fruitful forest. I have dug and drunk water, And with the soles of my feet I have dried up All the brooks of defense. "Did you not hear long ago How I made it, From ancient times that I formed it? Now I have brought it to pass, That you should be For crushing fortified cities into heaps of ruins. Therefore, their inhabitants had little power; They were dismayed and confounded; They were as the grass of the field And the green herb, As the grass on the housetops And grain blighted before it is grown. "But I know your dwelling place, Your going out and your coming in, And your rage against Me. Because your rage against Me and your tumult Have come up to My ears, Therefore I will put My hook in your nose And My bridle in Your lips, And I will turn you back By the way which you came. This shall be a sign to you: You shall eat this year such as grows of itself, And the second year what springs from the same; Also in the third year sow and reap, Plant vineyards and eat the fruit of them. And the remnant who have escaped of the house of Judah Shall again take root downward, And bear fruit upward. For out of Jerusalem shall go a remnant, And those who escape from Mount Zion. The zeal of the Lord of hosts will do this. "Therefore thus says the Lord concerning the king of Assyria: 'He shall not come into this city, Nor shoot an arrow there, Nor come before it with shield, Nor build a siege mound against it. By the way that he came, By the same shall he return; And he shall not come into this city,' Says the Lord. 'For I will defend this city, to save it For My own sake and for My servant David's sake.' Then the angel of the Lord went out, and [killed in the camp of the Assyrians one hundred and eighty-five thousand; and when people arose early in the morning, there were the corpses—all dead.

# Disciples Prayer in the Books of Acts

**Acts 4:24-31**

*So when they heard that, they raised their voice to God with one accord and said: "Lord, You are God, who made heaven and earth and the sea, and all that is in them, who by the mouth of Your servant David have said:*

'Why did the nations rage, And the people plot vain things? The kings of the earth took their stand, And the rulers were gathered together Against the Lord and against His Christ.' "For truly against Your holy Servant Jesus, whom You anointed, both Herod and Pontius Pilate, with the Gentiles and the people of Israel, were gathered together to do whatever Your hand and Your purpose determined before to be done. Now, Lord, look on their threats, and grant to Your servants that with all boldness they may speak Your word, by stretching out Your hand to heal, and that signs and wonders may be done through the name of Your holy Servant Jesus." And when they had prayed, the place was shaken where they were assembled together; and they were all filled with the Holy Ghost, and they spake the Word of God with boldness.

# David's Prayer of Thanksgiving to God

*1 Chronicles 29:10-20*
*Therefore David blessed the Lord before all the assembly;*
*and David said: "Blessed are You, Lord God of Israel, our*
*Father, forever and ever.*

Yours, O Lord, is the greatness, The power and the glory, The victory and the majesty; For all that is in heaven and in earth is Yours; Yours is the kingdom, O Lord, And You are exalted as head over all. Both riches and honor come from You, And You reign over all. In Your hand is power and might; In Your hand it is to make great And to give strength to all. Now therefore, our God, We thank You And praise Your glorious name. But who am I, and who are my people, That we should be able to offer so willingly as this? For all things come from You, And of Your own we have given You. For we are aliens and pilgrims before You, As were all our fathers; Our days on earth are as a shadow, And without hope. O Lord our God, all this abundance that we have prepared to build You a house for Your holy name is from Your hand, and is all Your own. I know also, my God, that You test the heart and have pleasure in uprightness. As for me, in the uprightness of my heart I have willingly offered all these things; and now with joy I have seen Your people, who are present here to offer willingly to You. O Lord God of Abraham, Isaac, and Israel, our fathers, keep this forever in the intent of the thoughts of the heart of Your people, and fix their heart toward You. And give my son Solomon a loyal heart to keep Your commandments and Your testimonies and Your statutes, to do all these things, and to build the [g]temple for which I have made provision." Then David said to all the assembly, "Now bless the Lord your God." So all the assembly blessed the Lord God of their fathers, and bowed their heads and prostrated themselves before the Lord and the king.

# Solomon's Prayer for Divine Wisdom

*2 Chronicles 1:6-12*
*And Solomon went up there to the bronze altar before the Lord, which was at the tabernacle of meeting, and offered a thousand burnt offerings on it.*

On that night God appeared to Solomon, and said to him, "Ask! What shall I give you?" And Solomon said to God: "You have shown great mercy to David my father, and have made me king in his place. Now, O Lord God, let Your promise to David my father be established, for You have made me king over a people like the dust of the earth in multitude. Now give me wisdom and knowledge, that I may go out and come in before this people; for who can judge this great people of Yours?" Then God said to Solomon: "Because this was in your heart, and you have not asked riches or wealth or honor or the life of your enemies, nor have you asked long life—but have asked wisdom and knowledge for yourself, that you may judge My people over whom I have made you king. Wisdom and knowledge are granted to you; and I will give you riches and wealth and honor, such as none of the kings have had who were before you, nor shall any after you have the like."

# PRAYER OF JABEZ

*1 Chronicles 4:9-10*
*Now Jabez was more honorable than his brothers, and his mother called his name Jabez, saying, "Because I bore him in pain." And Jabez called on the God of Israel saying, "Oh, that You would bless me indeed, and enlarge my territory, that Your hand would be with me, and that You would keep me from evil, that I may not cause pain!" So God granted him what he requested.*

1. Everlasting God, with humility and in deep reverence, I bow before Your holy throne as I come before the Courts of Heaven.
2. Father God, I thank You for hearing Jabez's prayer and turning his cursed life into a blessing. You are the God who overrules and changes our story.
3. I am confident that if You heard Jabez's prayer, You will hear my prayers too, and what You did for him, You are able to do for me. You are no respecter of persons.
4. Oh, that You would bless me indeed as You did for Jabez so that I can be a blessing to humanity.
5. Oh, that You would enlarge my life, my faith, my finances, my influences, my anointing, my vision, my creativity, my heart, my health, my knowledge, my wisdom, and my ministry.

6. May the Lord increase and multiply every area of my business, my houses, my properties, and my families. Enlarge my territory.

7. The Lord is a Rewarder of the passionate, the violent, the hungry and the diligent seeker.

8. That You would keep me from evil. Let no evil befall me. Let no curse, spell or hex have power over me. Shield and protect me from the attacks of the wicked. Raise a hedge of protection around me, a hedge that cannot be broken or penetrated by the enemy. Place a wall of fire around my borders. You are the God who answers by fire, so when the enemy comes knocking, may the God who answers by fire answer for me.

9. Barriers, limitations, hindrances, and restrictions are breaking today.

10. For the blessings of the Lord makes one rich and He adds no sorrow, grief or despair with it.

Thank You for hearing my prayers and for granting my requests. In Jesus' name I pray. Amen.

# OUR LORD'S PRAYER

*Luke 11:2-4*
*So He said to them, "When you pray, say:*

Our Father in heaven,
Hallowed be Your name.
Your kingdom come.
Your will be done
On earth as it is in heaven.
Give us day by day our daily bread.
And forgive us our sins,
For we also forgive everyone who is indebted to us.
And do not lead us into temptation,
But deliver us from the evil one."

# PRAYERS OF BENEDICTIONS – A SUPPLICATION OF DIVINE BLESSING

*Numbers 6:23-26*
*"Speak to Aaron and his sons, saying, 'This is the way you shall bless the children of Israel. Say to them: The Lord bless you and keep you; The Lord make His face shine upon you, And be gracious to you; The Lord lift up His countenance upon you, And give you peace, that you may walk in the light of God's love.*

1. May the Lord protect you from all harm.
2. May He restore whatever is broken within your life.
3. May the Lord show you His kindness.
4. May He reveal to you His mercy.

*Psalm 35:27*
*Let them shout for joy, and be glad, that favour my righteous cause: yea, let them say continually, Let the Lord be magnified, which hath pleasure in the prosperity of his servant.*

Your well-being comes from the hand of God, and it delights Him to bless you in that way.

May you feast upon the abundance of God's blessings and drink from the river of His delights.

2 Corinthians 13:14: The grace of the Lord Jesus Christ and the love of God and the fellowship of the Holy Spirit be with you all.

May the grace of God sustain you, give you purpose and allow you to be changed.

*Jude 1:24-25*
*And now to Him who is able to keep you from stumbling, And to present you faultless. Before the presence of His glory with exceeding joy. To God our Savior. Who alone is wise, Be glory and majesty, Dominion and power, Both now and forever. Amen.*

# A Tribute to My King Jesus

- ◆ In Genesis, He is my Light in the depth of darkness.

- ◆ In Exodus, He is my Salvation from every bondage.

- ◆ In Leviticus, He is my Jubilee and Yoke Breaker.

- ◆ In Numbers, He is my Shield and Anti-curse.

- ◆ In Deuteronomy, He is the Conveyor of my prophetic blessings.

- ◆ In Joshua, He comes into my life as a Captain of the Host of the Lord.

- ◆ In Ruth, He is my Cover and nearest Kinsman.

- ◆ In 1 Samuel, He is the Voice that called me by name unto Himself.

- ◆ In 2 Samuel, He is the Move of God in my life.

- ◆ In 1 Kings, He is the Wisdom of God and the Lion of Judah.

- ◆ In 2 Kings, He is the Manifestation of miracles that brings revival and resurrection upon contact.

- ◆ In 1 Chronicles, He blesses me and I am blessed forever.

- ◆ In 2 Chronicles, He shows Himself strong on my behalf.

- In Ezra, He is the Good Hand of God on my life.

- In Nehemiah, He is my Reminder and Restorer.

- In Esther, He is my Favor and Recompense.

- In Job, He does everything in my life, and no thought can I withhold from Him.

- In Psalms, He is the only Begotten Son of God through whom I possess the uttermost part of the Earth for His Kingdom.

- In Proverbs, He is my Wisdom and Principal.In Songs of Solomon, He transmits His sweetness into my mouth and makes me lovely like Him.

- In Isaiah, He is Emmanuel, my very present God.

- In Jeremiah, He sanctified me and ordained me as a prophet to the nations, and He blesses me with the performance of good things.

- In Lamentation, He manifests His great faithfulness and His mercies that never come to an end.

- In Ezekiel, He makes my face and forehead stronger than the faces of my enemies, and He brought me out of my grave.

- In Daniel, He is the fourth man and fireproof from the fires of the world.

- In Hosea, He is my Husband.

- In Joel, He is the Lord of my restoration and rain of

blessings.

- In Amos, He strengthens me against our strong spoiler.

- In Obadiah, He gives me the grace to possess my possessions.

- In Jonah, He commands the big fish to deposit me on dry land.

- In Micah, He is my Messiah come forth.

- In Nahum, He is my Good Lord and my Stronghold in the day of trouble.

- In Habakkuk, He is my Written Vision and Motivation for service.

- In Zephaniah, He confirms me as one of His remnant who shall see evil no more.

- In Haggai, He affirms His ownership of gold and silver, and He is blessing me from this day.

- In Zechariah, He is the wall of fire around me, and the glory of my life.

- In Malachi, He is my Refiner, Purifier who rewards my tithes with His abundance.

- In Matthew, He is my blood transfusion for a new life.

- In Mark, He commands me to preach the gospel to every creature.

- In Luke, He is my Dayspring from on high with a new dawn.

- In John, He is the Word that abides in me and makes all things possible for me.

- In Acts, He releases His Spirit to me by the baptism of the Holy Ghost.

- In Romans, He delivered me from condemnation.

- In 1 Corinthians, He is my Quickening Spirit who empowers me with the gifts of the Holy Spirit.

- In 2 Corinthians, He is my Triumph whose glory I behold, and He takes me from glory to glory.

- In Galatians, He is my manifestation of Holy character.

- In Ephesians, He is my Armor and Peace.

- In Philippians, He took me out of my mind and blessed me with His mind.

- In Colossians, He makes me consistent with His original plan for my life.

- In 1 Thessalonians, He calls me to sanctification and makes me rapture ready.

- In 2 Thessalonians, He recompenses tribulation to my troublers.

- In 1 Timothy, He is my King of kings and Lord of lords.

- ◆ In 2 Timothy, He reveals to me the Source of all Scriptures.
- ◆ In Titus, He saves me by the washing of regeneration.
- ◆ In Philippians, He is the location of every good thing in me.
- ◆ In Hebrews, He is the Heir of God who made me joint-heir.
- ◆ In James, He is the Father of Light with no variableness or shadow of turning.
- ◆ In 1 Peter, He is my Cornerstone and Chief Shepherd.
- ◆ In 2 Peter, He is my Source of excellent glory.
- ◆ In 1 John, He is my Advocate who destroys the works of the devil.
- ◆ In 2 John, He is my Source of truth and love.
- ◆ In 3 John, He calls me His well-beloved, and gives me the ability to proposer and be in good health.
- ◆ In Jude, He comes with ten thousand of His saints to execute judgment.
- ◆ In Revelation, He is the Revelator of Jesus, the Christ.

And Thank You, Lord Jesus, for being all this and more to me, now and forever. I recognize You and Your attributes with my own revelation. Amen.

# ENDNOTES

Igomadu, D., Breakingthrough Prayers: 2003.
New Kings James Version. Bible Gateway.
https://www.biblegateway.com/
Prayers For Breaking Generational Curses.
https://livingfaith.com/
William, Barbara. Prayers That Avails Much: Curse of Jezebel,
(Pg 105). 2014.

# ABOUT

Theresa Crichlow is the founder and visionary of Pressing into Prayer Ministries. Her vision is to reach as many people as possible with the gospel of Jesus Christ so as to expand the Kingdom of God. She is a seasoned prayer warrior, an intercessor, strategic prayer coach, and a healing and deliverance minister. She encourages believers to walk in the spirit, walk in authority, exercise dominion over the powers of darkness, and walk worthy of their calling. She activates gifts and empowers believers to do the work of the ministry through impartation.

Theresa has committed her life to the work of God by offering personal prayer support, mentorship, and life-transforming guidance to other believers across the globe. Her love for Jesus has birthed a deep burden for souls. This has resulted in the salvation of many and has brought about a positive impact in the lives of those she has come in contact with.

Whenever the opportunity presents itself, Theresa shares the principles of faith, which have become the driving force in her life and ministry. She has written a series of books on deliverance and prayer, as well as produced a Healing CD called "Divine Health."

In addition, Theresa is passionate about souls. She enjoys seeing the manifestation of answered prayers through intercession, according to the will of God. Her goal is to lead the efforts of God's body of believers to become more prayer driven.

God has also placed upon her life an unusual healing anointing, which has resulted in countless testimonies of miraculous healings and great deliverances. Her personal testimony consists of God raising her up from the dead after she had been kidnapped, raped and brutally beaten. Not only was she raped, she also suffered from the trauma of molestation and sexual assault all through her childhood.

Surviving a dramatic abortion attempt by her mother and being rescued again by the hand of God from suicide, Theresa's story is a display of a woman who now walks in her God-ordained destiny to set others free.

Despite all she has gone through and overcome, her journey of healing is not over. In fact, her testimonies have touched, healed, restored, and renewed the commitment of many lives. Her ministry is for those who have been wounded emotionally, as well as for those who have suffered one form of abuse or the other.

God has done amazing things for her and she is humbled by the ways in which the Lord has used and continues to use her as an intercessor for others, as well as in many other capacities.

In addition, she flows in a powerful prophetic anointing and releases the fire of the Holy Spirit, bringing fresh passion and a hunger for Jesus Christ. Sharing the principles of faith has become a driving force in her life and ministry.

She served for over 25 years in multiple areas of ministry in a church located in New York. She was active in the missionary community/outreach program, volunteered at the Bowery Mission Homeless Shelter, as well as various street outreach organizations, and she served as Community Relations Officer for a non-for-profit organization. Theresa was an assistant Sunday school teacher for toddlers, a key figure in the women's ministry, and co-president of the hospitality department. Upon joining the Prophetic Intercessor Ministry, where she received advanced training, she obtained a certificate in the Schools of Prophets. She also served as a head intercessor and adjutant for a prayer ministry which focuses on ministering to hurting women and creating a bond of true sisterhood. In addition, she also has a degree in Business Administration.

Being led by the Holy Spirit, Theresa joined an apostolic and prophetic movement that has gone global, serving as an adjutant intercessor and now as an executive administrator. In 2011, she was ordained as a licensed minister and affirmed as a Pastor where she served, and assisted in building a foundation for a prophetic prayer tower in the New York Chapter. She has also been involved on the board of numerous prayer and intercessory platforms throughout the years.

Theresa Crichlow is a native New Yorker. She is married to Wayne Crichlow, and through their union, they have been blessed with two sons.

9 781735 465449